# Working in Business and Finance

# Working in Business and Finance

*An Insider's No-Nonsense Career Guide*

Joseph A. Malgesini

BUSINESS EXPERT PRESS

*Leader in applied, concise business books*

First published in 2024 by
Business Expert Press, LLC
222 East 46th Street, New York, NY 10017
www.businessexpertpress.com

ISBN-13: 978-1-63742-612-8 (paperback)
ISBN-13: 978-1-63742-613-5 (e-book)

Business Expert Press Business Career Development Collection

First edition: 2024

10 9 8 7 6 5 4 3 2 1

# Description

**Demystify the fascinating world of business and finance.** This isn't your run-of-the-mill career guide; think of it as your secret weapon, your backstage pass to the good, the bad, and the ugly.

No more tiptoeing—we spill the beans on the pay, the hours, the perks, and the not-so-glamorous parts of the journey.

In this candid, concise, and comprehensive guide, we've condensed insider insights into a must-have manual for students and budding professionals. Whether it's consulting, accounting, investment banking, sales and trading, private equity, venture capital, investment management, hedge fund, real estate, corporate finance, strategy and operations, product management, sales, marketing, or getting your MBA, we've got it all covered.

We've thrown in candid conversations with real-life young professionals who've braved the same path you're about to embark upon. Whether you're a student mapping your future or a young professional hungry for success, this book will ensure you make career choices that you won't regret.

Replace career confusion with confidence by learning the ins and outs of the career paths available to you. **Your foray into a burgeoning career starts here**.

## Keywords

career guide; investment banking; finance; MBA; business; recruiting; job search; internships; consulting; accounting; hedge fund; private equity; real estate; product management; marketing; accounting; sales; strategy; venture capital

# Contents

# CHAPTER 1

# Introduction

The main goal of all those years you put into school is to help you get a job. But which job? Schools can be effective at teaching the minutiae, but often miss when it comes to teaching you what your career options are. At least, that was my experience. As a student with a general interest in business, I took all the classes, learned all the concepts, put in years of work, but then basically ended up aimlessly taking the first job that fell into my lap. I was "well educated," yet regretfully underinformed when it came to making one of the most important decisions of my life to date. So now, I'm laying out the information that I wish I'd known back then. If you have any interest in pursuing business as a career, studying economics, being an investment professional, going to business school, learning about consulting or sales or product management roles, and so on, then this is for you.

I'm going to lay out, as honestly and succinctly as I can, what your career options are after graduating college. The list is not exhaustive, and it is simplified for the sake of brevity and clarity. The way that I'm grouping and classifying these roles is entirely of my own making, but, that said, I hope to cover most of the options that are typically taken by ambitious young people with an interest in the world of business. I'll dive into what I believe the important considerations for each role are. That might include what the work is like, what the pay is like, what the exit opportunities are, what the lifestyle and hours are like, as well as some of my own opinions on the pros and cons of each one. While career centers or even other career guides might touch on some of these elements, they tend not to lay out all the roles together in one place and they often omit the kind of information, like pay, hours, or exit opportunities, that is of the most interest and use to students. My goal is to give you the inside scoop, with very candid takes, based on perspectives from people who have actually worked in these roles. For each section,

I will also include a written conversation with someone who either works or has worked in that role early on in his or her career. In order to learn about any career path, students are often encouraged to set up a "coffee chat" with someone who works in the industry so they can ask questions. My goal with these written conversations is to replicate those chats and save you some time.

I have an MBA from Columbia Business School, an MA in Finance from Claremont McKenna College, and a BA in Economics and Accounting also from Claremont McKenna College. The information and opinions that I'm laying out are largely based on the experiences that I, my peers, my classmates, and my coworkers have had, both recruiting for jobs and on the job. I leveraged my network to inform and provide feedback on the various sections that I will cover. The information I provide on these roles is only from experience in the United States, generally using New York as the standard. Things like salary, work–life balance, or company hierarchy may differ significantly in other countries.

Growing up, many of us are often told that you can be whatever you want. An astronaut, a firefighter, an investment banker, the list goes on. In business, while that's true up to a point, it becomes less so as time goes on. Once you choose what your first job will be, you are also choosing what it won't be, and thereby forfeiting options, often without even realizing it. That isn't to say that you can't change later on, but it will be much harder. If, after just a few months at your first job, you find yourself wishing you had picked something else, you might find that it is no easy task to correct that mistake. You're no longer able to apply through the school recruiting pipeline and, believe it or not, you are already branded by whatever it is you're doing. You may find yourself feeling stuck on a path that you don't want to be on and realizing that you've set yourself up for decades in a career that you aren't excited about. It can be scary. You can no longer just be whatever you want. Again, there are ways to pivot, but they are often more difficult than you might imagine. That is why it is so important to understand where your first job is leading you. All this to say that picking a first job is a huge decision. It's not just about your first job, it's about setting up your entire career to get you to where you ultimately want to be.

That is why I'd like to encourage you to take the exit opportunities of each role into serious consideration. It can be easy to glance over that and focus on starting salaries, but I assure you that isn't the right way to think about it. In the grand scheme of your career, your starting salary is not very important in and of itself. Of course, different people will have different priorities and perhaps making money immediately is understandably of more urgency to some than others, but just about nobody stays in the same job forever. The chance that you happen to pick the single most perfect role for yourself out of college is slim. Odds are, after two years, you'll find yourself fantasizing about another position or wondering where another path might've taken you. At that point, it won't matter how much you made those first couple of years. What will matter, however, is what opportunities are available to you next. And, on the off chance that you do stay in that first role for the long run, your long-term earning potential will matter much more than your initial salary. In the grand scheme of your career, what you make that first year is peanuts. While long-term earning potential and initial salary may go hand in hand, they won't always. Additionally, don't underestimate the importance of factors that cannot be put into a number. The fulfillment you get out of your work, the kind of people you work with, the lifestyle and balance that your role affords, and the skill sets you build are all important parts of the puzzle.

Let's back up to before you set your sights on business. To over-simplify it, here are, in my view, what your main career options are. You could go into law, medicine, engineering, government/nonprofit, or business. While there are certainly other options, like those which are more creative in nature, that may not fall into any of these categories, I tend to view these as the most common and, in this context, relevant five career paths.

With law, you'll probably take the LSAT, apply through a competitive selection process to law schools, attend law school for three years, take the bar for a specific state, and then find a job at a law firm. It will be a ton of reading, you'll need to be meticulous, and the hours can be grueling, but your eventual earning potential, depending on which type of law you choose to practice, can be very high, even ultimately in the millions.

Medicine means you'll likely become a doctor by taking pre-med courses as an undergraduate, studying for and taking the MCAT, applying to med schools, going to med school for four years, passing the medical licensing exam, matching with residency programs, completing at least three years of residency, passing an additional stage of medical licensing examination, getting board-certified through another test, applying for a state license, and then finding a job as a doctor. There are many different specialties with varying levels of demand and pay. Primary care physicians might make between $200k and $300k while specialists could make an extra couple hundred thousand. Pay will also largely depend on where the hospital is. It requires a ton of school, and while medical residents make some money, it won't be more than five figures. That said, being a doctor is likely to be very fulfilling. You serve a greater social good, help people for a living, make good money, can work anywhere (though it will probably have to be in person), and work hours that, while demanding, aren't likely to get too out of hand. There is a ceiling to what doctors within any given specialty will make. It's very good money but it won't scale to multimillions (unless you build a successful private practice) as could be possible in other career paths I'll mention.

Engineering is broad. You could be a mechanical, chemical, civil, or electrical engineer, just to name a few. A very popular choice these days is computer science. Folks with a computer science background are likely to become programmers, spending much of their careers at their desks working through code. Practically every company is a tech company nowadays, so programmers are likely to have lots of options with their computer science degrees. If they're able to land a job at a big tech company like Google, they'll have it pretty good. They can make close to $200k right out of college with great perks. That can double after well under a decade, and if they're able to keep climbing after 10+ years, it's sure to be upward of half a million. The job can be pretty cushy with reasonable hours, depending on the company, and will oftentimes offer remote work opportunities. It may tend to be an inherently less social role than others, but the skills acquired will set them up well for entrepreneurship should they choose to join the start-up world.

The government/nonprofit space could mean a lot of things. It's likely to be a path with ample purpose but limited pay.

Any of these four career paths could also intersect with business. Businesses need lawyers and sometimes those lawyers end up taking on additional business-oriented responsibilities. Health care start-ups may need doctors to help build products and market them to the right customers. Many government jobs have business counterparts, and lateral jumps are not entirely uncommon. Nonprofits are businesses in their own right and need employees that know how to run a business. Entrepreneurship along any of these paths will require business acumen as well. The point is that there are a lot of career paths that end up in the business world and, while some paths may be more limiting than others, it's helpful, whatever your background or interest, to understand what types of business roles exist.

That takes us to the last option on my list: business. I'm going to break business up into four broad categories and go deeper into the functions of each. In no particular order, there's consulting, accounting, finance, and industry.

# CHAPTER 2

# Consulting

Consulting in this context refers to management consulting, though even consultants have a hard time explaining what exactly it is that they do. They might work on corporate strategy projects or ones that are more operational in nature. Part of the appeal of management consulting is that consultants have the opportunity to explore all kinds of different projects and, depending on the firm, all kinds of different industries as well. The larger firms do work across just about every industry. You can go from helping private equity clients decide whether a particular investment in the health care space is a good idea, to restructuring the entire organization of an oil and gas company, to creating a go-to market plan for a retailer launching a new product, to trying to turn around a grocery business that is losing money. To give you a sense of the day-to-day, the first project example I just gave about private equity might include interviewing experts, building models to estimate the size and growth of the market, creating customer surveys, and performing competitive analysis. Both the industries and the functional areas feel endless and you will never stop learning as there is always something new to explore.

Consultants tend to work on high-impact projects where they will have the chance to interact with folks in senior roles, perhaps even the C-suite. Their clients might include Disney, Real Madrid, Chevron, or the government. The stakes can be high but that kind of exposure at a young age is difficult to find anywhere else. While it can sound intimidating or even ill-advised to be advising major clients on key business decisions with little to no actual experience as a new graduate, consulting teams are structured so that the experienced partners and team leaders make the big calls. Over time, you'll build a strong business acumen of your own and be able to contribute more and more to the problem-solving aspect of the job.

In terms of the day-to-day, consultants spend a lot of time in Power-Point preparing decks. You'll become adept at Excel as well, but unlike true finance jobs, the quantitative demands of the role are typically more limited. You will build a strong problem-solving skill set and a structured way of thinking that is highly respected in the business world. Leaving with a prestigious management consulting badge on your resume is sure to boost your job prospects down the line. While some firms expect a greater degree of specialization up front, others will give you time to explore and hone in on the type of work you'd like to focus on. Projects can be anywhere from a couple of weeks to many months. The lifestyle of a consultant can also be quite appealing, if you enjoy traveling, that is. Traditionally, consultants would be on the road Monday through Thursday, staying in fancy hotels near the client site and expensing all of their meals and transportation. While this still happens, COVID has lessened the amount of time that consultants, on average, travel. Consultants can indicate whether or not they want to travel, but sometimes, it will be out of their control. There may also be opportunities to travel internationally through specific programs, projects, or office transfers.

Consulting firms generally follow an "up-or-out" model. That means your promotion schedule is no secret. While folks might be promoted a bit early or a bit late, after about two years, you'll move to the next level. After around 10 or 12 years, assuming you join right out of school, you could be a partner. Partner is the highest level in consulting and the point at which you actually own a chunk of the company. If, at any point, it's decided that you are not going to be promoted, then you will be politely pushed out and told to seek employment elsewhere. A significant portion of the total compensation is your performance bonus, but first-year consultants stand to make about $135k all in. Two to three years later, it could be $220k, and if you stay a decade and make it to partner, it can be over a million, perhaps even a few million, with a huge chunk of that depending on how much business you bring to the firm. While that is obviously a lot of money, compensation in consulting will by definition depend on the number of hours that can be billed to clients. This "charge-by-the-hour" approach means that there is, so to speak, some sort of ceiling. I compare that to investing roles where compensation may be entirely uncapped. I should also note that at some firms, there is no cost-of-living adjustment, so the pay will be the same regardless of which U.S. office you work for. Your pretax dollar can stretch a whole lot farther in certain states.

Exit opportunities are abundant coming out of consulting. Many consultants will leave after a couple of years because they can jump over to a strategy, finance, or operations role, join a private equity fund, come in at a high level for a promising start-up, and so on. In fact, the top consulting firms will even have what are basically career counselors who are happy to help you find a new job. Most also have a revolving-door policy that means, assuming you left on good terms and it is within a reasonable number of years, you will be welcomed back to the firm if you later choose to return. Many firms will also cover the cost of business school for some of their consultants or give them the chance to do an externship, which is basically an internship at a different company while you are still an employee. It's also common for consultants to end up joining one of their clients. There is a vast network of ex-consultants that remain loyal to their firm and are often happy to not only give business to their ex-firm but also hire fellow consultants. Whatever the case, many doors remain open after a stint in consulting.

Consultants often choose to leave for a few reasons. The work can be tough and the hours can be grueling, depending on the project and the team, with nights going well past midnight. Such is the nature of being at the beck and call of a client. That said, work will almost never spill into the weekend. Consultants are also merely advisors. While they will make a recommendation, they generally don't get to stick around to see it through before they're onto the next project, which can be a detractor to some. Additionally, new job opportunities might just come up that offer better hours and similar or better pay.

The management consulting firms are generally grouped into a few buckets. You have the "Big Four," which are Deloitte, Strategy&, EY-Parthenon, and KPMG. You have the boutiques, which include LEK, AT Kearney, Oliver Wyman, Accenture, and OC&C. And, then, you have the group referred to as "MBB," which are McKinsey, Boston Consulting Group, and Bain. Within the United States, at least, MBB firms tend to be the most prestigious as they do a lot of high-level strategy work and charge clients a premium. The boutiques tend to be more specialized in terms of the kind of work they focus on, and the Big Four tend to do similar types of work as MBB but charge a lower rate. The Big Four also have a higher proportion of implementation work, meaning projects that implement proposed changes rather than focusing on the high-level strategic planning that comes before.

If you are interested in applying to be a consultant, you should seek an internship after your junior year and prepare yourself for case interviews. These are business puzzles intended to mimic real-life cases. You'll be tested on how you structure your thoughts, draw on business concepts, perform quick mental math, and communicate effectively. You'll want to get your hands on some mock cases and simulate an interview with someone who knows what they're doing. Cases could cover any industry or question, and while you will want to have plenty of reps under your belt, you don't need much technical preparation beforehand. Cases test common sense and basic mental math, not memorization or financial modeling.

There are no certification or licensing requirements. Consulting is also unique in the sense that there are no conventional background requirements. Experienced hires, that is, those who apply with existing post-undergraduate work experience, can come from all sorts of backgrounds. The same is true of MBA hires; all are welcome to apply. Consulting is a common path for MBAs who, at many firms, come in at a position that is effectively two to three years ahead of their undergraduate peers. Firms take some experienced hires, but recruiting off-cycle is difficult and there are not nearly as many spots as there are for on-cycle recruiting through the school pipeline. Regardless, it is competitive and will require significant preparation.

Consulting is a great fit for those willing to work hard in a high-stakes environment, comfortable with travel, hoping to see different industries, keen on keeping doors open, excited about building and presenting analyses, and interested in doing impactful work.

# A Conversation With a Consultant at Ernst and Young Parthenon

**What do you love about consulting and are there some unexpected benefits you've found the role to have that might not be advertised?**

*Coming out of business school, I still wasn't sure I knew the answer to the age-old question, "what do you want to be when you grow up?" Maybe, I wanted to start a company or be the CEO of a media company or pursue the dream of being a business journalist which I originally had planned when I started my MBA. I had very little idea of what a role with such a general title like "Consultant" really meant, but people had told me it was the "undecided major of careers," and I had liked the sound of that. All I really knew was that consulting would supposedly open many doors, and that was exactly what I was looking for. I've largely found that to be true. Although you may not always get your exact pick of projects every time, over the course of your career as a consultant, you have the ability to try different roles and work on a wide array of project types, industries, and functions. The degree of mobility you have will depend on the firm you end up at, and whether it is a "generalist" or "specialist" firm, but for the most part the major consulting firms like the big four and MBB are structured specifically to afford you a variety of experiences and opportunities. Even if you focus within a specific function or industry, you'll be working on all different kinds of projects. For example, in the last year that I've worked within our health care practice, I have yet to work on two cases that are truly alike or that focus on the same type of company. This means that I am learning every single day, and that keeps me interested and engaged in the job. I do truly feel that I am getting smarter through my work and building a valuable skill set that will help me in whatever future role I take on, whether that be returning to journalism, starting my own company, or even continuing in consulting. But, all of these are aspects of the job that consultants will advertise to you during coffee chats. There are also unexpected benefits, and though these vary by firm and function, they are relatively common for most management consulting firms. First and foremost, you get time on the "beach" or "bench" between projects, which is basically free time off when you aren't actively staffed. This is more abundant during slow times for the firms and becomes more of a rarity when business is booming, and you may get staffed on internal work during these times. But, all consultants do get beach time from time to time, and when you do it's pretty great. This is more common in practices where the projects are shorter (two to six weeks), since there are more opportunities for it.*

*I also like the dynamic nature of the job. Some projects will be lighter and easier and others will be more grueling, but since you change projects frequently, there's always an end in sight. If you don't like the topic or the team or the client, soon you'll be moving on to the next thing anyway. The day-to-day is also fairly dynamic. This isn't a typical finance job where you'll work long, set hours, or a banking job where you're juggling multitudes of clients and projects at the same time. Until you reach senior levels, at most firms, you'll be staffed on one project at a time. That means there are very busy days (before major deliverables are due), but there are also very light days scattered throughout the project, and that makes it feel more sustainable. As you get more projects under your belt, predicting these days can get easier, meaning you'll get to take more advantage of the down time. And it makes the late, busy days less tough, because it's not something you'll face every day for months or years on end.*

**Speaking honestly, what do you hate about the role? Do you have any regrets taking the role and why?**

*Between the strict, hierarchical structure and client-facing nature of the job, being a consultant can at times feel as if you don't have much agency. That can definitely be a frustrating part of the job—to some extent, you're always at someone else's whim or working on someone else's schedule. At the analyst (postundergrad) and associate (post-MBA) levels, your managers set deadlines according to when it is convenient for them to review. Sometimes, that means that you'll be working at inconvenient times, waiting around for a review during the day only to have to work late to turn comments if they don't get around to reviewing until the end of the day. Or, sometimes, you'll be crunching to get something done for a deadline that is somewhat arbitrarily set, which is usually okay and part of the job, but is the worst if your manager doesn't even end up reviewing during that time—good managers usually avoid this though. But, even at the highest level as a partner, you still serve clients and are somewhat at the mercy of their deadlines, demands, and schedule. And, when you're working for a client or partner who is a nightmare, or unreasonable, there's often very little you can do or say. Ultimately, whoever you answer to calls the shots and it's your responsibility to do as you're told.*

## What is the career growth potential like in the role?

*The great news about consulting is that it's an extremely structured hierarchy, with defined timetables and set progression, so you never really have to wonder about what's coming next. You don't need to worry that there won't be opportunities to move up or what role you might move into next because there always are and you always know. That predictability is great, but it also means that there is a pretty strong up-or-out model, meaning that you need to perform well (or at least to a satisfactory level) in order to stay in the role and move up the ranks. Consulting doesn't really allow for much stagnation. While you may be able to coast by for many years in another job as a lower-level performer, that doesn't fly in consulting. Generally, the performance standards get more demanding as you move up and the more years you have with the firm.*

*While that may sound stressful, the good news is that there is a strong culture of feedback, and organizational infrastructure that demands it on a fairly regular basis, so there aren't many surprises. You'll know when you're not doing well and be given direct feedback on how to improve. Though there is pressure, generally, the model provides comfort in knowing that there's always room to move up at the firm and that there's a distinct path for you to do so. And, if you do end up leaving, there are many doors open elsewhere as well.*

## What advice do you have for someone hoping to follow in your footsteps?

*Consulting is so much about the people. Do your due diligence to learn about the different cultures, values, and nuances of each firm, and make sure you're solving for fit when deciding between firms. There are slight differences between firms that impact a lot of the job like the ability to take vacation, work–life balance, and overall workplace culture. Make sure you weigh these carefully and think about what you need from your job to feel happy and fulfilled and what type of company you want to work for. When you're working in a demanding job like this, being at the right firm can make or break your experience and ultimately determine if you'll be successful. And if you're not a people person, I don't think you'll enjoy this job. So much of the job is team based, and being able to work well with people is a requirement to do well at the job and move up at your firm. If you are a people person, lean on that as much as possible and get to know the people on your team, in your practice, and at your company. You'd be amazed how far being warm, sociable, and willing to lend a hand will go in this industry.*

**What do you see as your most viable exit opportunities?**
*The exit opportunities coming out of consulting are numerous; it's a huge selling point of the job. You could move to an industry that you have done work within, for example, moving to Google as a consultant who has done some TMT (tech, media, telecom) work. This is one of the most common paths; so, if you're set on moving into an industry, it can be a good idea to focus on doing some work within that space. Tech, media, health care, industrials, government, education, consumer products and brands, and almost every industry you can think of are all viable options to exit to out of consulting.*

*You could also move into other finance roles such as private equity (PE) if you've worked as a PE consultant. Particularly at the postundergraduate level, many PE consultants exit into private equity roles due to the overlap in the work. PE is a notoriously difficult industry to break into, with set pipelines, and consulting to PE can be a smoother and easier path than investment banking.*

*Another attractive option is entrepreneurship or start-ups. Whether you're looking to found your own company or join an early-stage one, many consultants choose to exit to start-ups. Consulting gives you a unique toolkit that is well suited for this scene including understanding new markets, developing product strategies, improving operations, analyzing and solving business problems, and much more.*

*The best part about all of these opportunities is that if you leave on good terms, most consulting firms will welcome you back if you find yourself hating your new role. At my firm, I know several people who exited to industry, private equity and entrepreneurship only to find their way back a few years later. That's a pretty unique option compared to other fields and offers a level of safety and security to try new ventures.*

# CHAPTER 3

# Accounting

Accounting is the language of business, so becoming an accountant can make you well-versed when it comes to understanding financial principles.

It's highly recommended that you receive your Certified Public Accountant (CPA) license if you want to build a career in accounting. Doing so requires a certain amount of semester credits on relevant coursework. The specific requirements vary by state but they are no joke and often necessitate overloading on courses or taking an additional year of school to reach the threshold. Once reached, you can take the CPA exam which has four parts. In many states, you will have to complete all four within an 18-month window and less than 20 percent of candidates pass all four on the first try so it is no easy task. The four parts are Auditing and Attestation, Business Environment and Concepts, Financial Accounting and Reporting, and Regulation. You will also need a certain amount of professional experience, generally one year, before you can receive the license, so folks will typically work while they go through the CPA exam process. There will also be continued education requirements every couple of years in order to keep the license renewed.

The typical career path for an accountant would be to start at a Big Four accounting firm like Deloitte, EY, KPMG, or PwC as an intern after your junior year and then join full time. At that point, they will help you through the CPA process with reimbursements and incentives. These companies were mentioned in the consulting section since they all have consulting arms as well, but they are best known for accounting. There are, of course, many lesser-known accounting firms as well. The main accounting services that these firms provide are audit and tax, though many also offer advisory, risk management, assurance, and more. Audit means you'll spend your time evaluating the integrity and accuracy of a company's financial statements, ensuring that everything checks out and that transactions are correctly accounted for. Tax means you will help clients optimize their tax strategy and prepare their documentation.

The Big Four have the reputation of being sweatshops. Not unlike consulting, the hours in those first few years can be brutal. Accountants might work 40- to 60-hour weeks during the low season but can reach 70 hours during busy season weeks, with the occasional weekend compromised as well. Accountants can expect initial compensation, primarily composed of salary, of around $70k at a Big Four though it will depend on location and firm. This pay will increase modestly over your first few years.

While the initial salary is relatively low, the accounting firms will expose you to many different industries, give you a strong technical skill set, and allow you to manage people very early on. The Big Four also have offices all over the country which enables you to live just about anywhere, and you are likely to have some remote work optionality. Companies will always need accountants regardless of what's going on with the economy, so it is a safe career choice. The firms will generally help young employees get their CPA, and after that, many choose to leave.

Likely pivots that they might make include corporate accounting and corporate finance with the goal of working their way up the Chief Financial Officer (CFO) ladder. I'll touch on corporate finance roles later on but the corporate accounting path likely entails navigating your company through complex accounting decisions, preparing Securities and Exchange Commission (SEC) filings and other reports, establishing record-keeping processes, compliance, and so on. Controller is a position that these folks might aspire to, where they could stand to make anywhere from a couple hundred thousand managing a smaller P&L (profit and loss statement) up closer to seven figures covering a global P&L at a Fortune 500 company, though these would, of course, be the lucky few. An exit to a banking or investing role, as I'll also touch on later, is likely to require business school. If you decide to stay at a Big Four for the long run and can make it through the up-or-out culture, then you stand to make partner after about 15 years at which point the compensation becomes quite high. Partners are likely to break seven figures. It can be a grind at first with low pay and many hours, but at the finish line is a very cushy partner role.

Students might also go directly from college into an accounting role at a nonaccounting company though it is advisable to start at an accounting firm. The badge and the experience offered by a Big Four or similar such company are likely to be an important part of building a career in accounting. Just like with consulting or banking, having a strong brand name and the resulting skill set from a prestigious firm will hold some weight and open up more doors for you if you choose to leave after a couple of years. The Big Four will do that. It will be fast-paced, you might be required to travel, and you will see faster career growth. Accountants can also make a good living in industry roles (i.e., at nonaccounting companies) where the work is likely to be repetitive, the hours are likely to be good, and the job is likely to be routine. Accounting is not a role that MBA students go into.

If you're someone who is meticulous, technically inclined, willing to work hard, and interested in either a partner role at an accounting firm or the finance organization in an industry role, then the accounting track might be a good fit.

## A Conversation With an Audit Professional at Deloitte

**What did you love about the role and were there some unexpected benefits you found the role to have that might    be advertised?**

*First, career timeline. My favorite thing about public accounting was the accelerated pace at which you gain experience/responsibility. In my third year at Deloitte, I was managing the day-to-day of teams of up to four to five staff and leading meetings with senior members of my client's accounting and finance function. It could definitely at times feel like being thrown into the deep end and having to learn to swim on the fly, but overall I think that early exposure was huge in my development. I don't necessarily think that level of exposure is common across other industries or within the private accounting industry. I think this remains a theme throughout your time in public accounting as you rise up the ranks—where you don't have to be on the lookout for external career advancement opportunities, because there is a natural internal progression.*

*Second is co-workers. Another benefit to public accounting was the relatively young age of the people you are working with. For the most part, you are working with co-workers who are in their 20s, and much of your day-to-day training is with co-workers two to three years older than you. In public* accounting, you spend a lot of time with your team, so the young vibe on the teams made it a lot more enjoyable and made learning on the job a lot less intimidating. I am not exaggerating when I say that currently some of my very best friends are former audit co-workers and bosses. I was actually just at my former manager's bachelor party a few months ago.

Third is a predictable schedule. I do think a benefit of public accounting is the predictable nature of the schedule. I can't sugar coat the hours, they can be a lot and busy seasons do suck—but if you are interested in public accounting, I assume you are looking at other roles where they are going to work you pretty hard as well. The benefit to public accounting is that you know for the most part when your busy periods are going to be and when your workload is going to be light. For example, if you're on a public client that files their 10-K on 12/31, you are going to be busy from January to February each year, and in April, July, and October following their quarterly filings.

Fourth is paid time off (PTO). I understand that this probably isn't a make-or-break item in determining your career path, but I don't think I have any friends/colleagues in other industries that have as many available PTO days or as little pushback against taking PTO days as I did in public account-ing. As long as you book your days in advance and don't try to take PTO during busy season, you are able to very easily book relatively large chunks of PTO and there is little risk that you will be asked to move it. This is absolutely not the case in other industries.

**Speaking honestly, what did you hate about the role? Do you have any regrets taking the role and why?**

As mentioned above, there are pros and cons of the audit schedule. The con that gets talked about the most is busy season. For two to four months at the beginning of each year, your life is basically working and sleeping from Mon-day to Thursday. Then, depending on your client and the status of the audit, you may get a normal Friday and weekends free, or you may be working the entire weekend. During this time, most Big Four firms have a no PTO policy, so there's no ability to take trips or have much of a structured social life during this period. There is also the possibility of being put on a client whose fiscal year-end is on 3/31, 6/30, or 9/30—which means that your busy season cor-responds with that timing. In my experience, this generally means having some *additional busy season months added to your schedule, as opposed to being a replacement for the traditional busy season beginning in January each year.*

*There is a recurring element of monotony to the role. By nature, there are a lot of rather tedious "check the box" exercises that are required throughout the performance of an audit. These are generally given to first years and sometimes second years. As such, in your early years, there can be monotony in your day-to-day. As your career progresses, this day-to-day monotony does die down as you are frequently given increased responsibilities and more challenging tasks. However, I personally did start to develop a feeling of year-over-year monotony, where you get used to the overall audit cycle (i.e., busy season, audit planning, quarters, interim testing, prebusy season prep, busy season, etc.), and that began to wear on my motivation.*

### What is the career growth potential like in the role?

*As touched upon above, I think the career growth potential is definitely one of the benefits of the role. If you are confident that public accounting is what you want for your career, there will be a very visible upward path within your firm, and you have the opportunity to get relatively consistent, frequent feedback as to where you stand along that path. On the other hand, if you are somebody, like myself, who graduated from college with the general idea that you wanted to be in accounting/business operations/finance fields, but were not necessarily sure where within those fields you wanted to end up, audit provides a solid training ground that keeps your external options open in the first few years of your career. That said, these options do start to narrow the further up the chain you go within audit.*

### What advice do you have for someone hoping to take the accounting path?

*I have two main pieces of advice for someone starting a career in audit.*

1. *Try your best to find people you enjoy working with and do your best to get under their "staffing umbrella." Many first and second years put too much emphasis on getting staffed on specific clients that they think seem interesting from the outside (i.e., I like movies so I will do whatever it takes to get staffed on Paramount). While there's definitely a "coolness" aspect to this initially that charm eventually wears off and, at the end*

*of the day, audit is audit. I found that the overall experience at each client was totally dictated by the people on your team. I would rather be staffed on a client that I've never heard of with people I trust, who trust me, and whose company I enjoy, than on a seemingly "cool" client with people I don't work as well with. Not only does this make the long hours more manageable, but from a career/mentorship standpoint, I cannot overstate how beneficial it is to have bosses who know you on a personal level, want to invest in your growth, and are willing to go to bat for you from a performance/scheduling standpoint. So, if you do find yourself on a team that you're comfortable on and enjoy, let your seniors/managers/ partners know that and do your best to get staffed on their other jobs.*

2. *If you do end up deciding that audit isn't for you, which is common, be intentional about your exit and make sure that you are running toward something you are interested in as opposed to just running away from audit. Big four firms have tons of resources—whether that be related to placing you externally or transferring you internally—that aren't available to you once you leave. Attrition is common and expected. The staffing structures at these firms would not work if it wasn't. In my experience, the attitude toward people leaving is positive and your partners will often go out of their way to make sure you understand your options and may even leverage their network to help you get where you want to go. Don't let fear of backlash get in the way of the resources available to you.*

### What do you see as the most viable exit opportunities from public accounting?

*There is no shortage of exit opportunities from a career in audit. As already touched upon, the overall structure of audit firms plans for and actually relies on a certain level of exits as auditors rise up the ranks.*

*The most common external exits for people early in their careers were seemingly to accounting and financial analyst roles within the private sector. However, I had former co-workers leave after one or two years to a variety of roles—including investment banking, strategy consulting, sales, and data analytics. As you progress within your career, the more common external exits morph accounting manager, assistant controller, controller-type roles, or VP of accounting-type roles.*

*Another very common exit strategy is an internal transfer to a different service offering within your firm. Big Four firms offer a huge variety of services and will often work to retain high-performing employees by offering internal transfers (from audit to tax, advisory, mergers and acquisition (M&A), etc.) or internal rotational programs where they allow you to spend time in one of these other roles with the option of returning to audit following your rotation. These can be great for people who enjoy working in professional services but have determined that maybe audit isn't the best fit for them long term.*

# CHAPTER 4

# Finance

## Investment Banking

Investment banking (IB) is often regarded as the holy grail of entry-level jobs when it comes to finance. This is not to be confused with commercial banking which deals with your everyday checking and savings accounts. While banks like JP Morgan or Bank of America offer a whole host of services, IB itself typically refers to a subgroup of those services. Investment banks act as financial advisors to companies. The most common topics on which they advise are mergers and acquisitions (M&A), equity capital markets, debt capital markets, restructuring, and leveraged finance.

IBs will often charge a small percentage of the deal size in fees to make money. However, given the size of deals like Amazon's acquisition of Whole Foods or Facebook's Initial Public Offering (IPO) (each over 10 billion), a small percentage of fees can amount to a large sum of earnings for IB teams.

Investment banks are structured into "product" groups and "coverage" groups. Neither is necessarily better; it just depends on your personal interests. To simplify, think of the two most common product groups as M&A and capital markets.

M&A groups advise either a seller on the sale of their business or division of their business (sell-side deal) or they advise the buyer on the purchase of a business or division of a business (buy-side deal). Either way, you will represent your client in a broker capacity and help facilitate a fair deal. This may involve finding counterparty buyers or sellers, structuring the sale, conducting valuations, negotiating a good price, advising on terms, and so on.

Capital markets groups help companies raise cash by issuing equity, which includes IPOs (initial public offerings), and by issuing debt. Either way, capital markets groups find investors, advise on capital structure decisions, set prices, ensure regulatory compliance, and so on.

Coverage groups specialize in a particular industry like technology, health care, consumer and retail, etc. If you're interested in a particular industry, then you may want to consider a coverage group. Here, you'll become an expert in that industry and work on both M&A and capital markets deals, albeit not as in-depth as if you sat in a product group.

Regardless of your group, as an entry-level investment banker, you are likely to spend a lot of time financial modeling in Excel, preparing pitch books to help sell work, and conducting various research tasks.

I'll start with the bad. The hours are the worst of any job mentioned here, perhaps any job period. Entry-level bankers might work around 80 hours each week with some weeks surpassing 100 hours. The norm is likely to be six- to seven-day workweeks, which means that you are on, all the time, night and day, seven days a week unless you have a certain period protected on the weekend. Even worse, a good chunk of that time will be spent with nothing to do, waiting in the office for work to come back with comments that you'll have to address. Picture sitting around from 8 p.m. to 11 p.m. only to then receive work that will keep you occupied well past midnight. The culture has a reputation of being cutthroat. Banks are increasingly adamant that you come into the office rather than work remote, you'll have to dress up more than in other roles I've mentioned, and much of the work, early on at least, will be tedious, repetitive, and unfulfilling. Demand for bankers can also be very economy dependent so a job in banking is not the most secure.

On the bright side, the pay is great (though perhaps not on a per hour basis). First year out of college all-in pay is likely to be somewhere around $180k in a city like New York though it will differ by tier of bank. The bonus makes up a huge portion of the pay, often between 50 to 100 percent of the salary, which is worth noting because, in bad years with low bonuses, you could stand to make significantly less. In the second year, you will see a pay raise of maybe $20k but then the pay starts to scale much more rapidly than consulting does near the middle of the ladder. The truth is most people leave around year two; the hours get to them, and they decide to do something else. After a couple of years of IB, you will have tons of great exit options, perhaps more than in any other role I'll mention. Private equity (PE) is a particularly common exit, and many bankers will even interview for PE during their first year of banking. PE can offer slightly better pay and lifestyle. It should also be of note that PE funds recruit almost exclusively from investment banking analyst classes, so if you are interested in PE as a career option, IB (particularly M&A or leveraged finance groups) will give you the most straightforward path to break in. Other common exits include hedge funds, venture capital (VC), and asset management (AM), as well as industry roles like corporate development, treasury, investor relations, strategy, and financial planning and analysis (FP&A). Some may also join or launch a start-up or pursue an MBA. I will touch on all these later on. IB is the ultimate job for launching a career in business as you will be highly sought after and just about every door will be open to you. Having the banking badge on your resume shows that you are intelligent, well trained, and capable of hard work. With all these great exit opportunities, it is no surprise that so many leave after just two years, but if you are one of the few who choose to stay, you stand to make a lot of money. You could become an MD (managing director) after about 15 years at which point you might make between $1m and $3m, potentially comparable to what consulting partners make though highly dependent on a variety of other factors. Just like in consulting or accounting, at the partner-equivalent level, much of your compensation will depend on the deals that you bring to the company. MDs take home a chunk of the deals they bring in, so the pay could certainly be higher than $3m in a good year. The hours supposedly improve at higher levels, so MDs won't be working quite the backbreaking hours that their analysts do.

Getting a job in IB is extremely competitive. You basically need to start positioning yourself for it during your freshman year of college. The most successful candidates I know worked at some sort of investment manager during the summer after their freshman year and then applied for banking roles at small banks during their sophomore year summer that would set them up for banking roles during their junior year summer that would turn into full-time offers. While you don't necessarily have to do it that way and while banks don't mandate that kind of experience so early on, it certainly helps keep you in the game amidst such a competitive field of applicants. The top-tier banks are generally looking for applicants with top of the class caliber GPAs at target schools like Ivy or Ivy equivalents. It will require a lot of hustle, preparation, and luck. The interview process is technical. Sources like Wall Street Prep can help you prepare for them. You will need to learn about the three financial statements, how they relate to one another, how to build certain financial models, and much more. If you do secure a full-time banking role, you'll have to pass a few licensing exams shortly after starting work. IB is also a common post-MBA role where MBA graduates come in at the associate level often breaking $300k in total compensation during their first year.

Banks are generally divided into three categories. You have bulge bracket (BB), middle market (MM), and elite boutiques (EBs). BB banks are huge and global, and they do just about everything with the largest companies in the world. They include Goldman Sachs, Morgan Stanley, JP Morgan, Bank of America, Citigroup, Barclays, Deutsche Bank, and UBS. MM banks are much like BB, but they work with smaller companies and can be focused on particular regions. MM includes firms like Jefferies, Houlihan Lokey, and William Blair. Boutiques can also do large deals, but they tend to be more specialized in terms of their services, industries, or regions. EBs often pay substantially more than BB or MM firms. Boutiques include Centerview, Evercore, Lazard, and Moelis. The most sought-after roles are typically at the top BB banks or the EBs.

If you are someone who is quantitatively inclined, not afraid of crazy hours or expectations, interested in the high finance world of Wall Street, and eager to maximize your earning potential, then IB might be a good fit.

## A Conversation With an Investment Banking Associate

**What do you love about IB and are there some unexpected benefits you've found the role to have that might not be advertised?**

*A lot of IB is using accounting and finance to break down and value companies, usually in Excel. I love this aspect of the job and it's probably what I do most often.*

*I'd also say I love the camaraderie that comes from working with my team for long hours at a time. Every deal, I'm on a team of four to six people ranging from analysts up to MDs. When you work the late nights and weekends that we do, you naturally develop strong relationships to get through each project.*

*I also love being able to see a tangible result to the work I do. There's a lot of preparation, stress, and uncertainty behind most IB deals. So, when the deal goes through, there's a real sense of accomplishment there. You can also directly see the value you added to your firm and to your clients in the closing of that deal.*

*Finally, as a generalist associate, I get to work in all kinds of industries and learn a lot about how those businesses are run. For example, I'm on an agri-industrial deal learning about fruit production and distribution across the world. On the other hand, I'm also diving into the media space as I'm on a deal with a smaller family-owned television company in Latin America. In a deal process, bankers usually work and develop relationships with senior management at these firms, which is not normal for someone in the earlier stage of their career.*

*One unexpected benefit in banking is the relationships you'll make across the buy side and at regular corporations. The turnover in banking is high with most analysts, associates, and even more senior employees moving to PE, hedge funds, and often corporate strategy departments of client companies. Banking is a very social job and the longer you stay in the field, the larger your list of contacts will be across the street.*

*The other benefit I would mention is travel. It's not always glamorous destinations as an analyst or associate but you often fly for site visits, management presentations, and general due diligence for your clients. As you get more senior, you also fly more to other offices across the world for joint projects. It is usually not mentioned but there is a lot more travel in banking than most realize.*

### Speaking honestly, what do you hate about the role? Do you have any regrets taking the role and why?

*At times, I hate the nature of how the teams operate. At lower levels, most of your job is waiting on guidance from your managing directors. As an example, your managing director may meet with a client at 1 p.m. and then have calls until 5 p.m. He/she will then send to you at 5 p.m. what the client wanted, and they want the deliverable by the end of the week. So, you spend the evening working on the deliverable and send out a first draft that night. However, your MD can't or doesn't look at it until 5 p.m. the next day and sends back comments again around 6 p.m. So, you stay late again to make those changes to the deliverable. This process continues until you send the deliverable to the client. I often find myself wasting my mornings and afternoons waiting for comments that don't come until late in the day which forces me to stay up late working on them.*

*My only regret is that I didn't get into IB sooner. I joined as a post-MBA associate and have been really enjoying the work. However, if I had joined out of undergrad as an analyst, I would be much farther along in my career. I'd also say that the experience you get as an analyst is different and, in some ways, more valuable than the experience you get as an associate. Analysts are focused more on the model and Excel, which builds a great foundation for a career in IB or even PE and hedge funds. Other than that, I don't have anything I regret with the role.*

### What is the career growth potential like in the role?

*There's actually a lot of career growth potential in IB. As I mentioned before, turnover is very high. But, turnover is high more because people choose to leave for other fields and not necessarily because they are let go. Essentially, if you decide to stick it out, you will progress up the ladder. Sometimes, just being available is more important than capability and in banking, this is often true. The main risk to growth would be a market downturn where deal flow stops, in which case you could be let go.*

*However, the promotion to managing director is where career growth does start to change. As a late-stage VP or director, you need to be able to generate business and close deals to get promoted and get paid. At that point, it's not enough to have stuck around; you need to have the skill and relationships to close deals.*

### What advice do you have for someone hoping to follow in your footsteps?

*As I mentioned before, get into IB as early as possible if interested. Undergrads usually recruit in the spring of sophomore year. Keep that GPA as high as possible and try to do something finance and deal related the summer of your freshman year. Use all contacts you have when recruiting. Utilize your schools' resources and programs that send students to IB. If you're coming from MBA, get into the best school you can and recruit aggressively for an associate role the fall of your first year.*

*In terms of the actual job, study corporate finance, accounting, and Excel in as much depth as you can. These three topics are very important to the job itself. The job will be much easier the more knowledgeable you are on these topics.* Wall Street Prep *and* Training the Street *have some great courses if you can afford them.*

*Try to get in the habit of following financial news. Read the* Wall Street Journal, Barron's, *or* Financial Times. *Have a viewpoint on what's going on with interest rates and the economy. Be aware of some of the larger deals happening in the economy. All of these will help you stand out when you are recruiting and when you eventually join a firm.*

*Network and look for mentorship as much as possible. If you're not sure about IB, reach out to anyone from your school to ask questions. This will help you make sure it's right for you. Once you're on the job, mentors and connections can help answer questions or get you out of bad situations.*

*Last thing, your attitude is very important on the job. Everyone is working long hours, and everyone is stressed. But, not everyone can stay positive while working. When it comes time for performance reviews, the people with good attitudes consistently outperform the people with bad ones.*

**What do you see as your most viable exit opportunities?**
*Almost all analysts in IB leave after two years to join PE firms. A smaller percentage leave to join corporate development or strategy departments at larger firms as well as investing roles at hedge funds. As an analyst, exiting into these roles is pretty common. As an associate, exiting into corporate development is most common but there is still opportunity to join a PE or hedge fund. I'd say the most viable opportunities are opportunities related to whatever deals you were working on. For example, if you worked on a lot of deals in the tech space, then you'll most likely exit to a tech-focused PE fund or a tech firm like IBM and Google.*

## Sales and Trading

If you've ever seen an old video of Wall Street folks running around yelling and trying to place orders on the trading floor, that's sales and trading (S&T). At least it was. It's quite a bit less hectic nowadays but the concept remains. S&T is a group at investment banks that connects buyers and sellers of financial instruments. The term often used is market maker. When investors want to make large transactions, they will often go through S&T to help them find a counterparty and the S&T desk will take a commission. This is agency trading. S&T might also serve as that counterparty by buying or selling on behalf of their own bank if the price and risk profile are right. This way, the S&T desk can profit off the bid–ask spread. This is principal trading.

It could be stocks, bonds, currencies, commodities, and so on that are being traded as well as derivatives of these assets. Those who work in S&T are effectively both middlemen and investors. That means the job can be pretty intense. So long as the market is open, you have to be on, and your track record is easily measured in terms of how much money you made or lost for the company on any given day so the stakes are high. As you rise through the ranks in S&T, you might receive more responsibility and freedom in terms of the trades you make but you will likely always be selling and trading, even at the MD level. It requires you to be very attuned to the markets and you'll be making quick reactions rather than working on long-term projects.

S&T hours are better than IB hours as you'll be in lock step with the stock market which is open 9.30 a.m. to 4 p.m. EST or the bond market which is open slightly longer. You'll come in before it opens and leave after it closes though you'll also have to stay up to date on news. You also generally won't have to work weekends. The compensation for analysts and associates is at a slight discount to banking as first years will make somewhere around $145k all in. S&T compensation is extremely performance based and so pay can fluctuate drastically by firm, employee, desk, and year. That makes it tough to even ballpark what MDs in S&T make but you can use IB compensation as a proxy and assume it's in the millions. In S&T, you will likely learn a lot about how the markets work as well as the various financial instruments traded on them.

The exit opportunities from S&T are much more limited than those from IB. Many folks leave after a year or two in S&T. The most typical exits would be hedge fund or AM. I'll touch on these down the line. They are great options, but it really locks you into a specific career path. As electronic trading has picked up, the role of S&T has become less import-ant over time. As machines continue to get better at making markets and executing trades on behalf of the banks, S&T may continue to fall by the wayside though it is likely to be needed for addressing clients that want to interact with a person as well as for more complex transactions and illiquid assets.

Interviews for S&T are likely to evaluate your knowledge of and interest in markets and financial products as well as throw some brain teasers at you. This differs from banking which might test accounting or valuation principles. Firms tend to seek out students with more of a math, finance, or computer science background as the work can be rather quantitative. Computer science has become much more valued in recent years.

Students will generally apply to the S&T divisions at the BB banks though there are also some trading roles intended for new grads at quantitative trading firms like Jane Street or SIG. These can be particularly prestigious and will only take the best and brightest math minds around. First-year quantitative traders at Jane Street take home over $300k though Jane Street would certainly be at the high end for those kinds of roles. While these "quant" roles do have some functional and product overlap with S&T, they are much more coding and modeling intensive, so the entry-level hires tend to have a computer science skill set. At the experienced hire level, quantitative trading firms might recruit software engineers, PhDs, physicists, and those with MS (Master of Science) degrees. I'll touch more on buy-side quants in the investment management/hedge fund section but will also note here that quant roles exist at banks as well serving as effectively a support function for the S&T folks. These quants also typically come from a computer science background but will fall below S&T in the pecking order.

Generally, students will intern their junior summer at a bank and then receive a full-time offer from a specific S&T desk. Each desk handles a certain product like fixed income or equities and may be further specialized beyond that. Interning during your sophomore year summer will only boost your odds. Most interns receive return offers but networking across groups can be an important part of the process. Once you join full time, you will need to pass some licensing exams. MBA students do not recruit for S&T roles.

If you are mathematically inclined, enjoy competition, and are set on devoting your career to the markets, then S&T could be right for you.

## A Conversation With a Sales and Trading Professional

**What do you love about sales and trading?**

*Today was payroll, a very important data point for the markets. When the data was released at 8.30 in the morning, it was a big surprise for markets. I heard 200 people on the floor screaming and jumping—not sure if all of them were happy, but sure all of them were impacted by the data one way or another. S&T is among the most exciting jobs in finance. You're not involved in markets—you ARE the market. You provide prices and liquidity to clients, you make your own decisions very early on in your career and you take risks by yourself—either good or bad, the decisions are yours as are the consequences. You can choose how to think about anything—you want to be a fundamentalist trader on corporate bonds? Sure. You want to use graphics and technical analysis? Why not? You want to be a quant? More than welcome—as long as you think by yourself and develop your own ideas and skill set. Trading is a career where you eat what you kill—and it doesn't really matter how you do it.*

**Are there some unexpected benefits you've found the role to have that might not be advertised?**

*Very very regular hours. You get in at the same time every day, you get out at the same time every day. You have full weekends to enjoy as you like. You get to have a routine and have a life outside your work—which sometimes can be hard to find in high-paying jobs in finance.*

**Speaking honestly, what do you hate about the role? Do you have any regrets taking the role and why?**

*It's very flow based. The routine can be really boring if clients are not doing much—you depend on outsiders to trade and to make money. You can spend time reading, developing models, and polishing your other skills, but the core is trading and that's totally dependable on what the buy side is doing and if they are including you in their quotes and conversation. Also, it's a heavily political place—you need allies and people who support you to grow in your career—more than in other places. No regrets taking the role so far, I like it very much—it's very intense during the day, but it's worth it.*

**What is the career growth potential like in the role?**

*There's very little rotation in trading roles. People who get a good desk tend to stay for very long—it's very good pay, interesting work, and ok hours. What else do you want? Growth potential can be stellar if you are a killer—you can make a lot of money as early on as associate and you trade your own book. It's very P&L based—I know some associates that are making more than VPs just because they have a better P&L. Also, becoming a managing director over time is doable—stick around, have a good track record, be good to those around you. Other than that, a lot of traders are hired by hedge funds and then the sky's the limit. I have personally known a few traders who made the move to the buy side and are doing pretty well. Developing a certain set of skills in S&T and then using them at a hedge fund is a great career move.*

**What advice do you have for someone hoping to follow in your footsteps?**

*Keep curious and follow markets. Develop coding skills like Python and Excel skills. VBA is great and usually underestimated nowadays. Apply yourself to understand what's happening in the world and how that may affect the markets you're interested in. Try to focus on one market to develop a better knowledge of a few products and of its dynamics. As an example, do you like economics? Try to understand bonds, treasuries, futures contracts and settlement dynamics, and so on and how they are affected by Fed policies, inflation scenarios, and current geopolitical events. That will help you to stand out as someone that is not only interested in markets but also willing to put in the hours and work to really develop a deeper knowledge of finance and what's going on.*

**What do you see as your most viable exit opportunities?**

*Stay around and become a director and managing director or make a move to a hedge fund and try to make money on the buy side.*

# Private Equity/Venture Capital

PE and VC are two of the most lauded career paths in finance. Basically, what they do is raise money from investors and then invest it into private companies. They are both known for traditionally charging their investors 2 and 20, that is 2 percent of the total assets under management (AUM) and 20 percent of profits. This makes them lucrative businesses and they are therefore highly competitive to get into.

### Private Equity

PE firms invest in more mature businesses. They buy a large stake in the target company with a combination of cash from investors, or limited partners (LPs), and debt that they will pay off with the cash proceeds from the business once they own it. That's why they call it an LBO or leveraged buyout. Leverage refers to debt. Firms build a portfolio of companies for each fund and attempt to sell them at a profit maybe five or so years after buying them. There is an element of value creation during the period of ownership where the PE tries to cut costs and/or grow revenue. This means that the investment is much more hands-on than just picking a stock and that some operational know-how is key. Some funds have operating-specific roles whereas others will have the investment or deal team handle that. Acquiring other companies is also a common component of the value creation stage. This means tucking in or adding on an additional company to the initial investment and the more junior employees often get very involved in the execution here. PE groups will generally have members of the deal team added to the board of directors for quarterly board meetings and strategic planning. Junior folks at the fund might attend board meetings as observers.

PE typically hires people with IB experience. The most traditional route would be banking for two years, PE for two years, maybe an MBA (though in many cases it isn't necessary), and then back to PE. Consultants may also be considered for roles but, as a general rule, banking is the path to PE and it will be significantly harder without a banking background. Finding a PE job straight out of undergrad is very uncommon but not entirely unheard of. The larger firms might offer them and the pay for those roles will probably be less than what IB analysts make. Most people join in their mid-20s as associates and stand to make between $300k and $400k at one of the larger funds or closer to $250k at a smaller one. Bonus makes up a huge chunk of that, even up to 200 percent of the base salary. After the associate level, it becomes more likely that you will be given carry, which is a cut of the profits or the 20 percent that I mentioned earlier. Some funds might also offer coinvest which gives you the chance to invest your own money in one of the deals. If you stick around for the long run and make partner around the time you're 40, you stand to earn anywhere from one to a few million a year all in. This is highly variable based on the fund size and performance since carry will represent a huge portion of what you take home. If some of your deals are home runs, then you could have years where you make much more.

Interviews are likely to include LBO modeling tests or requests to pitch a potential investment, though the focus will probably be on prior deal experience from your time in banking, if applicable. Because it is less common for students to join PE directly from college, there is not a very structured pipeline like there is for banking, consulting, or accounting. Recruiting will require a lot of hustle in terms of preparing yourself for interviews and reaching out to contacts to set up chats. This will be the case whether you're applying directly from college, as an experienced hire, or as an MBA student.

Associates in PE spend a lot of time on market research, engaging with the management teams of portfolio companies, and leveraging financial models. The work is generally considered more interesting than banking and the hours might hover between 60 and 70 per week, which also beats banking, though can still be grueling. PE is seen as an exit in and of itself but, if you choose to leave PE, common options would be going to a hedge fund, a VC firm, a corporate strategy role, or even running one of the portfolio companies. Some folks might also try to start their own PE fund. One way or another, there will be doors open to you.

PE firms may also have operating roles. Some will be more "back-office" jobs that handle things like reporting across the portfolio while others will be more hands on in the value creation and growth processes at the portfolio companies (portcos). This can be an interesting option for those with operating experience like consultants or industry hires who want to get into the PE world. Some of these roles will also have more overlap with the investment team than others so it is important to clarify what the responsibilities will be before joining. Another role at many PE shops is business development. These folks do deal generation and may serve more of a sales function than a finance one since they spend significant time doing cold outreach. With this role, it would also be important to clarify exactly what the responsibilities and career progression opportunities would be. While both can be compelling ways into PE, they likely will not sit on the same pedestal as the investment team and may be viewed as slightly more "back-office" roles. Some firms may also have executives in residence (EIRs), though they may go by a variety of other names, who are basically more senior operators, like ex-CEOs, that will work with one or several portcos during the holding period. Alpine Investors is an example of a firm with a renowned EIR program.

There are a couple of other PE variations that are worth mentioning. Growth equity is a term you might hear thrown around. Think of it as very similar to PE but you are taking a smaller stake in less mature companies with faster growth and you are focusing more on driving growth to create value. It sits somewhere on the spectrum between PE and VC. In terms of careers in growth equity, for all purposes here they will look very similar to what was mentioned for PE.

There are also search funds which follow a relatively similar approach to PE. They bring on searchers who will spend sometimes up to two years finding a company for the fund to buy and then running that company by themself. Searchers usually have quite a few years of experience under their belt or are coming off an MBA and want to run a company but not start one from the ground up. Search funds present an opportunity to do this though they will take a sizeable chunk of equity away from the searcher. Alternatively, a searcher can circumvent the fund entirely by raising money, finding, and then buying a company solo.

PE funds will have varying theses or areas of focus. Some might invest exclusively in health care while others might be climate funds. If you have expertise in a particular area that is relevant to a fund, that will boost your odds of breaking in. There is also real-estate PE (REPE) which deserves its own mention here because it is different in the sense that rather than investing in companies you are investing in properties. I'll dive deeper into real estate in a later section.

If you are financially inclined but also interested in operating businesses and doing deals with uncapped earning potential, then PE could be a great fit.

## A Conversation With a Private Equity Professional

**What did you love about the role, and were there some unexpected benefits you found the role to have that might not be advertised?**

*I wholeheartedly enjoy investing in private markets companies, which is why I believe I am well suited for PE. Not everyone enjoys investing, and those who do enjoy it may like other types of investing over PE (e.g., public markets hedge fund investing and VC). There are a lot more moving pieces in PE than other types of investing, given that you are acquiring a company, but that's one of the things I enjoy most about the role—it always keeps things interesting. An unintended positive benefit that you get from working in PE is built-in exit opportunities through working with portfolio companies. After your fund acquires a business, the company is owned by the fund which has complete control over hiring and firing. If it's a company that you'd be excited to work at and there is a business need for you and your qualifications to work there, then it becomes a very easy conversation to have. It's not something that is typically thought about, and certainly not a reason for working in PE in the first place, but it is an unintended benefit that people don't typically realize until working in the industry.*

**Speaking honestly, what did you hate about the role? Do you have any regrets working in PE and why?**

*No regrets. I've always enjoyed my time working in PE, which is also why I decided to go back into it after business school. The chief complaint I typically hear from my friends working in PE who may have more regret is that they went to a fund that wasn't aligned with what they were looking to do—for example, someone who wants to work in a lean, entrepreneurial environment, but accepts a job at a mega-fund (hundreds of investment professionals, >$5–10 billion AUM) or someone who wanted to work on big, market-moving deals but is at a lower-market fund and only works on very small deals. It may sound like it's all the same, but there are big differences in terms of the actual job and responsibilities across the industry, and if it doesn't align with what you are looking for or what your strengths are, then it won't be a good match and you may have regret.*

**What is the career growth potential like in the role?**

*Career growth potential is dependent on the fund you are at. As a junior deal team member working at a fund, your ability to grow into a more senior position will look very different depending on the type of fund you are at; for example, someone who is joining a newer, leaner fund would have a much different experience than someone joining a mega-fund with hundreds of investment professionals. It is not that dissimilar to any other type of work environment from that perspective.*

**What advice do you have for someone hoping to follow in your footsteps?**

*My advice would be to put in the work and be prepared. You never know when someone will give you a shot, whether that be to have a networking conversation, interview, and so on. You want to make sure you are putting yourself in the best position possible and a large part of that includes being prepared— for example, practicing LBO modeling and studying the technical finance questions that one could expect being asked in a PE interview. There are a lot of interviewing guides out there that are helpful resources. Second, I would caution you to make sure you are choosing PE for the right reasons (i.e., you actually enjoy working in finance, working on deals, etc.). The people who burn out or don't end up doing well in the job are those who primarily chose the profession for the wrong reasons (like wanting to make a lot of money). It's hard to compete and excel at the job if you don't truly enjoy it.*

**What did you see as your most viable exit opportunities?**

*Similar to IB, I think PE lends itself well to many exit opportunities. This could include going to work at an operating portfolio company (as described earlier), other types of finance/investing roles (credit, secondaries, etc.), investor relations/fundraising roles, or many other types of roles/opportunities.*

### Venture Capital

VC is the younger brother to PE. VCs invest in start-ups and are generally quite tech focused. They tend to take a minority share, write smaller checks, and have higher risk/return profiles than PE firms. VCs expect most of their investments to fail but count on having just a few bets pay off in a big way. They place bets on the idea and the leadership of a start-up whereas PE can base bets on prior performance and just switch out the management team. Most of the start-up success stories that you've heard of were funded by VC. Silicon Valley is the homeland of VC though the start-up ecosystem has, over time, expanded beyond just the bay area. Venture capitalists tend to have a love for investing and innovation and will spend substantial time meeting with entrepreneurs and envisioning the future.

PE really exists on a spectrum ranging from angel investing to early-stage VC to growth equity to PE. Notice that PE generally refers to one end of that spectrum, though technically it defines the whole spectrum since it all involves equity in private companies. Some VC funds will participate in all stages from pre-seed or seed all the way to Series E or F while some might only focus on early or late stage. Some have a sector focus like climate or health care while others might have a technology or business model focus like business-to-business Software-as-a-Service (B2B SaaS) or frontier tech. There are fund of funds that might look like VC but really just invest in other VC funds. There are venture studios which launch start-ups in-house. There are incubators and accelerators like Y Combinator which effectively offer membership and support to start-ups. There are corporate VC arms like Google Ventures which invest in start-ups on behalf of their parent corporation, and then there are the more conventional VCs. For recruiting purposes, it's important to be aware of the differences.

Some of the top VC funds are Andreessen Horowitz, Sequoia Capital, Kleiner Perkins, and Bessemer Venture Partners. Much like PE, it is very difficult and not that common to join a VC fund right out of college. There is minimal structure to getting a job in VC and there is no archetypical background either. They will hire engineers, entrepreneurs, PhDs, experts from different fields, bankers, consultants, and MBAs. Whichever level you come in at, hustle is the name of the game. You will need to do lots of networking and have some investment pitches ready to go. Going deep on a sector by becoming an expert and building a network can make you a more compelling candidate. If you are, instead, more of a generalist, you are more likely to need a strong pedigree coming from an Ivy or a top bank, for example. Many VC jobs are not posted anywhere, and hiring will be done directly through the fund's network. It is a long game in the sense that just because you may not be able to break in at a certain level does not mean that you can't break in later on. VCs will be especially friendly to folks who have worked in the start-up world and had successful exits. Most folks at the analyst level may have worked at a start-up or in banking, consulting, or product management for a couple of years and then joined the VC. They're likely making below $100k and are spending most of their time doing diligence. Often, they are not on a partner track and may even be expected to leave the VC after a couple of years.

A level up the ladder is the senior associate role, though terminology might differ by firm, where you might make between $120k and $200k depending on the size of the VC. This is the post-MBA role and carries with it more interesting work and a higher chance of sticking around at the firm. Associates will spend a lot of time meeting with founders, researching topics, and bringing opportunities to the higher-ups. The hours in VC might be around 60 per week, with weekends generally off, though they can get crazier in the heat of a deal. There is a lot of net-working and you'll be attending many events, so if you don't enjoy that, then this may not be a great role for you. Becoming a partner is especially challenging in the VC world. Some VCs will make it clear that you are on a partner track, meaning that if you stay at the firm, the goal is for you to become a partner. In other roles, the expectation will be that you do not ever become one. Partners often join laterally after having a successful exit rather than working their way up the ladder.

At the partner level, you are sure to have carry and your pay will be extremely dependent on the size and success of the fund. If the fund hits a home run, then your compensation could be well into the millions but it could also fall well short of a million. It's a fool's errand to try and put a single number to it. Partners are well paid, the ceiling is limitless, and earnings overall tend to be more variable than in PE.

As mentioned, there is not exactly a typical path to VC. Your best bet to get in early may be to work for a start-up, as a banker, or as a product manager, which I'll discuss later, for a couple of years and then try to join at the associate level. If you're able to launch a company and sell it for a bunch of money, then that might get you in as well! VC, like PE, is considered an exit opportunity so if you want to leave, you will probably go to another fund, join a start-up, or launch your own start-up.

It's also worth noting that there can be a lot of variance between VC roles. There are two dimensions that drive this variance. One is stage, whether it's pre-seed, seed, series A, series B, and so on. The job of a seed or pre-seed investor is wildly different from that of a series B investor, for example. The other dimension is the type of work. Every firm operates differently in terms of the type of work junior investors do. Some firms, like Insight, are sourcing shops where the name of the game is coverage and cold outreach to as many companies as possible, as early as possible. Some firms, like USV, are very thesis driven and focus a lot more on thesis development (research, reading, writing, and internal discussion). Some firms work with a smaller number of companies and are "lead investors" able to work closely with their companies. Other firms write smaller minor checks and/or have massive portfolios and can't really support their portfolio much. All this to say, be sure to really do your research on each firm.

VC is a great fit for those interested in investing, keen on networking, and particularly excited about innovation.

### A Conversation With a Venture Capital Professional

**What do you love about VC and are there some unexpected benefits you've found the role to have that might not be advertised?**

*Every day is a new day. One day, I am doing deep research about zero-knowledge cryptography, the next day I am learning about modular nuclear reactors, and the next day I'm talking to a founder about the future of autonomous agents. It is nonstop learning in many directions. At my firm specifically, the role is very much choose-your-own-adventure. It is about following your curiosities wherever they may go.*

*One unadvertised benefit is probably access to smart people. I think it is advertised that you get to talk to really great entrepreneurs, but I have also found myself in the room with authors, politicians, lawyers, professors,* and seasoned non-CEO operators. This is partially a function of the firm I work at which has a big brand and network, but it is decently generalizable. I think the role of VCs is to be deeply curious and I think nontech people like hearing from VCs what they're seeing and investing in. The combination makes it easier and more credible to get in front of these kinds of folks.

**Speaking honestly, what do you hate about the role? Do you have any regrets taking the role and why?**

*No hates, some dislikes:*

1. *Most of the job is passing on founders. It is not enjoyable to have to tell people no so much. You also have to say no tactfully such that you are being honest, helpful, and thoughtful but also keeping the door open for potential future investment. If you pass on the seed, you may do the A; if you pass on the A, you may do the B.*
2. *There are no explicit feedback loops in this job. To know that you are good at this job requires consistently bringing in/advocating for good deals. To know that they are good deals and to see consistency (such that you weren't just lucky/unlucky) takes 10+ years. So, it is very hard to know if you are good at the job; the only thing you can do is try to constantly refine your process (instead of focusing on outcomes), but even then it is nonobvious that those process efforts are directionally correct since there is no feedback.*
3. *VC is a hits-based business; 80 percent of bets entirely fail, then 15 percent have middling outcomes, and 5 percent are true home runs. The net result is that a single great deal can really make your career. VC can have outlier financial outcomes, but it requires at least 5 to 10 years, and often more.*
4. *The job has the potential to color your interactions with others in a negative way. You are constantly "on" and, in theory, any interaction could, in some winding path, lead to a great deal. I see a lot of junior VCs that come across a bit less genuine or have a very transactional demeanor or style of communication. I think this is, in part, a product of the types of people pursuing these jobs, but it is also a product of the job itself.*

*Definitely no regrets though, I love my job.*

## What is the career growth potential like in the role?

*It depends on the firm. Most junior VCs do not stay in their role more than two years. Some firms have a path to partner (which would be the goal if you stay in this role). Some firms do not have a path to partner. In such cases, it is common for junior investors to make lateral or diagonal moves to another firm.*

## What advice do you have for someone hoping to follow in your footsteps?

*There are no required paths into VC. I know a VC from almost every possible background/previous job/college major. There is only one thing required: context.*

*My advice would be, to whatever extent possible, to do the job before you get the job. If you're interested in VC, you must already have some passion/interest around some areas of technology. Cultivate that interest by reading books/tech blogs that are relevant/interesting to you. Build a point of view on a couple of different areas. Writing is a great way to hone and demonstrate your thinking.*

## What do you see as your most viable exit opportunities?

*The most common paths out of VC are:*

1. *Operator, like strategy, finance, product management, or software engineering at a tech start-up.*
2. *More VC, either at a different firm and/or a different stage. It's not terribly uncommon for people to start their own funds.*
3. *Founder. VC helps with this in the sense that you get exposure to a lot of different areas and ideas. This can be helpful in finding the idea that is right for you. It can also help with understanding how to fundraise well and how to tell a good story. But, these are only small benefits and being in VC doesn't really impact your chances of success that much. It is also an exit path that you can take from any job, so it is not something uniquely unlocked by venture.*

*I don't think VC unlocks any career paths in the same way that IB, PE, and consulting do. There are very few hard skills that you learn in this job. I generally only recommend VC to those who think they might want to do it for a long time. Otherwise, there are much easier and more fun paths to becoming a good operator/founder.*

## Investment Management/Hedge Fund

There are a variety of career choices to be made within the world of managing money. It can get pretty nuanced and the nomenclature can be confusing but let's simplify it and think of it like this. There's AM, there's hedge fund, and there's wealth management. There are, of course, many other investment careers as well, some of which have been mentioned already, but for all intents and purposes, by "investment management/hedge fund," I'm broadly referring to these three.

AM firms may invest in various financial instruments including bonds, stocks, Exchange-traded fund (ETFs), and real estate and the main goal is to maximize return while minimizing risk. They can help investors build portfolios that match their risk tolerance. They are generally less risky than hedge funds, more regulated by the SEC, and they charge lower fees. This makes them safer and friendlier for unsophisticated individuals hoping to invest their money. In addition to portfolio managers, some AMs use robo-advisors to construct portfolios, that is, algorithms to choose how the capital is invested.

Hedge funds, in comparison, are much riskier, less regulated, and more expensive than traditional/broad asset managers. The goal is to maximize returns often through the use of leverage. Hedge funds are only available to accredited investors. They might take more concentrated speculative positions and implement more complex strategies.

Wealth management is a more holistic approach to managing money where individual investors can receive help on their tax strategy, estate and retirement goals, and portfolio construction based on an individual's specific risk profile and personal preference. Wealth managers will often invest capital indirectly through an asset manager, though they could also invest some directly. Wealth management firms are often smaller family offices, though banks may also have wealth management divisions.

If any of these roles sounds interesting, a job as a research associate would be a typical starting point for you. The role of research associate, or comparable roles perhaps by different names, exists on both the buy side and the sell side. Roles can be found at banks, AM firms, hedge funds, research firms, and more. For some reason in this space (and not in most others I've covered), "associate" often refers to those coming right out of college while analyst is the step above. The two main types of research associates are credit and equity. Both of these can exist on either the buy side or the sell side. While it is great, and considered a bit sexier, to get an entry-level job on the buy side, the sell side is more common for undergraduates. Equity research associates are in the business of finding investment ideas in the equity of publicly traded companies or deciding whether to buy or sell a stock. They will generally be assigned a coverage universe, including a handful of companies within a specific sector or industry such as retail, transportation, or interactive entertainment and hunt for new investment ideas through market research, company due diligence, and financial statement and valuation analysis under the watch of analysts. Analysts will be more involved in writing the research reports, contributing investment ideas, and interacting with the management teams of companies in their coverage. Credit research associates, on the other hand, tend to be even more technical and will evaluate items like a company's capital structure, credit or interest rate risk, and bond covenants. For the sake of simplicity, I'll focus on equity research here.

Students interested in this path commonly come right out of college and work in equity research roles at investment banks or AM firms where they might work 60-hour weeks with an early start to their days (often before 7 a.m. in credit and 7 to 8 a.m. in equities), though the hours can get much worse during earnings season, particularly on the sell side. In their first year, if they're at a BB bank, they stand to make somewhere between $125k and $160k all in, a discount to investment bankers but with better hours. This discount can become more pronounced at senior levels with MDs likely shy of or just scratching a million, though this, of course, depends on factors like seniority, sell side versus buy side, role, and firm. On the sell side at banks, equity research generates information that is used by bankers and traders but does not, in and of itself, drive much revenue relative to other divisions. After 1.5 to 4 years, many equity researchers, if on the sell side, will transition to the buy side to an asset manager or hedge fund. If already on the buy side, one can be promoted to a more senior research position with a larger coverage universe or work toward a role as a portfolio manager which might be a 5- to 10+ year process. Some might also use an MBA or perhaps a chartered financial analyst (CFA) to help facilitate that transition. The CFA test has three levels, typically takes three years to achieve, and requires a significant amount of studying (300+ hours per test). Passing can help bolster your career prospects across the investing world and may even be required for certain roles. PE and VC are less likely exits as those tend to look for the kind of deal experience that investment bankers have and equity research associates do not, though it does happen occasionally.

Bridgewater, Citadel, and Point72 are examples of top hedge funds while T. Rowe Price, Fidelity, and PIMCO are examples of top AM firms. Whichever path you choose, there is an option to pursue the role of portfolio manager, though this path is sure to be competitive. You might join an AM firm around the post-MBA analyst level and be making around $300k all in. Hedge funds will likely pay a bit more though with greater volatility based on performance, lower job security, and a more intense environment. AM firms generally offer better hours. Again, pay here is difficult to even ballpark because there will be a huge range. At the upper echelons of a large AM firm or hedge fund, pay can be in the multiple millions with hedge funds offering the highest earning potential in the space though it is sure to be variable year over year. A bad year could mark the end of a given hedge fund while a good year could provide a life-changing windfall. The compensation at both AM and hedge funds includes an annual salary potentially between $200k and $600k, an annual bonus that is performance driven anywhere from half of your salary to multiples larger, and sometimes longer-term retention incentives. AM and hedge funds are viewed as exits so if you choose to leave one of those, it is likely that you're just switching to another fund or perhaps starting your own hedge fund or family office. The work in either case is likely to involve company filings and financials, financial modeling and valuation, sell-side analyst and company management meetings, industry and macro-economic research, and investment strategies, though the strategies are likely to be relatively similar across AM firms while less conventional and more varied across hedge funds.

I should also note that there are both discretionary hedge funds and quant hedge funds. Discretionary hedge funds are what I've been referring to so far as they focus on company fundamentals and human judgment. This scope of work is a logical evolution from something like equity research. Quant hedge funds rely on computers to digest data and systematically make trades based on algorithms. As I touched on in the S&T section, this quant career path is likely to start with computer science or data science while experienced hires might also come from fields like physics or graduate degrees like master's or PhD in finance and computer science. The quant path can be very lucrative (with starting compensation over $300k at certain firms) though it can also be cut-throat in the sense that poor performers won't last long. Quant is seen as an exit in and of itself so subsequent roles would likely involve a similar scope of work within the hedge fund world. As the industry continues to become more tech driven, the distinction between these two hedge fund types may become less clear.

If you have a passion for picking stocks and conducting research and are willing to put in tough hours in exchange for great earning potential, the investment management path could be a good fit for you.

### A Conversation With a Buy-Side Equity Research Analyst

**What do you love about equity research/investment management, and are there some unexpected benefits you've found the role to have that might not be advertised?**

*This is a job for the intellectually curious and intrepid thinker. You are basically getting paid to learn something new every day. If you are passionate about investing, you can always find a new business to learn about or a new piece of information you unearth that helps your thinking.*

*It's also very rewarding that you are constantly talking to the leaders of the industry you cover. Whether that's the CEO or CFO of a public company, the senior sell-side analyst that covers the company, or experts/consultants who have years of experience working with the company that you're doing research on, you get to learn from the best of the best. If you can do this at an early stage of your career, treat it as a gift.*

**Speaking honestly, what do you hate about the role? Do you have any regrets taking the role and why?**

*There's honestly nothing I hate about this role, otherwise I wouldn't still be doing this job; however, if you're the personality type that likes to be told what to do by your boss and deliver definitive work, this is not the right job because in investing, the buy/sell decision is never a permanent one as the market is constantly evolving and your job covering a specific investment never ends. You also have to be creative and disciplined at the same time in knowing how to make your own schedule. Analysts are given a lot of autonomy for their work, but if you're not putting enough effort in, it'll eventually catch up to you.*

### What is the career growth potential like in the role?

*Most investment managers have a very flat structure where it's the (1) portfolio managers who are in charge of making capital allocation decisions on both sector- and stock-specific levels and (2) analysts, who are either generalists or sector specialists, who generate investment ideas for different strategies. At some of the larger firms, you may begin your career as a research associate, where you start learning about equity research by doing some of the more basic modeling and note-taking tasks supporting a senior analyst. Some people like to stay as career analysts because they prefer the research part of the job, while others want to graduate into a PM role and make capital allocation decisions. You also tend to do more client-facing work as a PM so make sure that's an aspect you're comfortable with.*

### What advice do you have for someone hoping to follow in your footsteps?

*Be honest with yourself about whether this is the right job for you. Unlike a lot of other occupations, an equity research analyst never really stops working because there's always something going on in the market. If you are taking a walk in the park on a Saturday morning, would it be painful for you to put on your air pods and listen to a company's earnings call or an investor podcast?*

*Be detail oriented and have long-term vision. I believe this is a job where you need to not lose sight of the forest but also pay close attention to the tree in front of you. There are so many factors that go into investing: market growth, company fundamentals, share gain, margin movement, capital allocation, management incentives, macros, valuation, and so on. Every single factor could move a stock. More often than not, only 20 percent of these factors drive 80 percent of what matters for an investment. The problem is, if you aren't aware, especially as a younger analyst, of how all these factors come together to make or break a stock, it's impossible for you to arrive at a well-informed investment decision. So, early on in your career, it's always more helpful to do as detailed work as possible, but at the same time build your knowledge of what might be the most important drivers for each business.*

**What do you see as your most viable exit opportunities?**
*This is an industry known for its low turnover because many people treat it as a lifelong career, including myself. If you're a fresh out of undergrad young professional, banking or consulting would probably be better for you if you're looking to use this job to pivot into something else. Not to say it's never happened, but you'll have a better chance getting a PE or corporate development job with banking/ consulting over equity research. For buy-side research, if people do get out, investor relations/fund of fund/ endowment types of roles are more typical on the margin, though the skill set you gain in this job will really differentiate you from many of your peers. Of course, if you do very well, you can always build enough wealth and retire to manage your own assets!*

## Real Estate

I'm giving real estate its own section because it is unique. While several of the roles within real estate, like IB and PE, share a lot of similarities with the traditional IB and PE roles already mentioned, the truth is that real estate is something of its own world with its own specialized ecosystem.

It offers compelling career opportunities with many roles to choose from. Let's break it into five different roles for the sake of simplicity. There's brokerage, lending, IB, PE, and development.

A real-estate broker (think real-estate agent or realtor) helps connect buyer and seller and takes a percent of the sales price as commission. Becoming a residential broker is a sales role at heart and is typically not seen as particularly prestigious. Top residential brokerages include Keller Williams and Coldwell Banker and the compensation on a path like this will be very much based on how much you sell. That said, there are also more high-profile roles at large commercial real-estate firms like CBRE, Eastdil, or JLL that stand to offer more robust exit opportunities. These roles might be more technical, even taking on something of an advisory role, thus making the leap into PE or development more realistic.

Lending is an interesting and often overlooked opportunity. Some of the larger commercial lenders are banks like Wells Fargo and JP Morgan and they offer roles that are less competitive than some other roles I've mentioned and so more accessible to folks from nontarget schools. These roles involve reading through appraisals and doing market research, evaluating the financial situation of the borrower, performing real-estate financial modeling, structuring debt, and so on. At a more reputable firm, you will earn less than bankers, perhaps close to or just shy of $100k out of school, and work tough hours that could likely exceed 60 per week, but you will have outsized exit opportunities within real estate that could include PE.

IB is more of an advisory role supporting real-estate companies on large transactions, namely M&A, and capital raising. I won't elaborate too much because the role is much like the M&A and capital markets roles already described in the IB section. The pay and the lifestyle are similar as well. REPE would be the archetypical exit. You can find these roles at the big banks as well as many of the boutiques.

REPE is basically the same as traditional PE except that instead of buying companies, you're buying real estate. The basic idea is you raise capital, buy properties, improve them, and then sell them for a profit. There are also real-estate investment trusts (REITs) which are functionally very similar to REPE but with a different capital raising structure and certain tax advantages. There are typically two kinds of front office roles within REPE: acquisitions and AM. They are somewhat self-explanatory: acquisitions make the investments and asset management deals with the properties post acquisition. Acquisitions tend to be the more prestigious and more lucrative role, though both are well respected. There are more ways into REPE than into traditional PE and they include banking, lending, development, and real-estate AM, though the main avenue into an acquisitions role would still be real-estate IB.

An acquisitions role will entail conducting market research, modeling new opportunities, traveling to properties, working with legal teams, and so on. As always, there is huge variability in pay depending on many factors but think of the compensation and career progression as being similar to those of traditional PE. Firms like Blackstone, Oaktree, and Brookfield lead the way in the REPE space.

Finally, development is the more entrepreneurial sibling to these other paths. It involves raising money, buying real estate, developing it, and then selling. There are no prerequisites or required previous experiences. Anyone can, in theory, do it. It is high risk, is high reward, and will require you to be very hands-on across every stage, including working much more closely with the actual construction team than you would in any of the aforementioned roles. It is an exciting path and might become a more realistic option once you have some relevant experience under your belt.

One added benefit of a career in real estate is the opportunity to leverage your knowledge to invest your personal wealth in real estate. Acquiring rental properties is a common approach to building passive income, and having experience in real estate will give you a leg up if you choose to do that. On the flip side, it's worth noting that a career in real estate can limit your opportunities to pivot. Real estate is particularly specialized and is a bit siloed. You'll learn a ton about things like real-estate markets and development but that knowledge doesn't carry over so easily to other industries. Just know that if you stay in real estate for very long, you might find it increasingly difficult to get out.

Real-estate finance might be appealing to those who are interested in the traditional banking/PE route but prefer dealing with a more tangible and straightforward product.

### A Conversation With a Former Eastdil Real-Estate Investment Banker

**What did you love about real estate investment banking, and were there some unexpected benefits you found the role to have that they might not advertise?**

*The best part about working in real-estate IB is the responsibility you are given at a young age. Eastdil is a place that emphasizes training by doing. You will not be working on case studies or work that is not material. Almost all the work you do will be directly sent to clients on live deals or prospects. From your first year, you will be given intense training and expected to provide material value. There are designated teachers to aid your technical development (financial modeling) but you will be the one running the numbers of the deals. Because of this, you begin to gain a comprehensive understanding of what makes a deal work or not and what investors look for. One of the things that I did not think about, but turned out to be a huge value add, is the emphasis on creating a story of the deal. I knew there was going to be intense technical training and emphasis on modeling knowledge, but being on the IB/broker side of the business forces you to understand the story of the real estate, and not just the bottom-line numbers. You need to focus on market drivers both from a real estate and a capital perspective, which I find to be important as it is easy to get stuck in the numbers and forget the context of a deal as an analyst. Another aspect that is not advertised is the network of young professionals you develop by working in commercial real estate at a young age. There is a huge emphasis on knowing the other analysts in your area from other companies. I am very close friends with a multitude of people I worked with at Eastdil and other close clients during my time.*

**Speaking honestly, what did you hate about the role? Do you have any regrets taking the role and why?**

*No regrets, but it is incredibly intense, and you will need to focus most of your time and energy on work. I knew what I was getting into, but it was exhausting both physically from the hours and emotionally as you will have to get used to starting projects without having full knowledge of how to get to the final product (we called it "changing a tire while driving 70 mph"). It was certainly hard at points but honestly incredibly rewarding and set me up both professionally for my next role and also in terms of confidence. When you are pushed as hard as they push you, you walk out with a sense of pride and accomplishment that you can tackle any task. If I had to do it again, I would do the exact thing.*

**What is the career growth potential like in the role?**

*It's hard to compare as I can only speak from my experience and for my expectations. I will say this without going into too much detail: most analysts have their choice of jobs whatever company they want to work at after their two years as an analyst. I loved my team at Eastdil so I stayed on as an associate.*

*I was lucky to be offered an opportunity I could not pass up to take a senior position at a debt fund. I was not actively recruiting because I loved the team I was on and still felt I was learning and being pushed in year three. When a couple of Eastdil's largest clients heard I was leaving, they reached out and sent me offers just on the reputation that Eastdil had.*

**What advice do you have for someone hoping to follow in your footsteps?**

*Choose a first job you are going to be pushed at and learn every day. Find something you are genuinely interested in and work really hard at it even if the environment is intense. Pressure makes diamonds.*

**What did you see as your most viable exit opportunities?**

*Eastdil has a reputation for placing their people at fantastic next opportunities. Again, I was offered a unique position I was excited about but everyone who goes through the Eastdil program essentially has their pick of PE firms after a few years.*

# CHAPTER 5

# Industry

Industry, as it is used here, refers to the business-related roles that are more industry agnostic. These are "in-house" or internal roles that typically exist at any company. A consultant who leaves his MBB job might move to industry in a strategy role at Amazon. An accountant who leaves her Big Four role for industry might be joining Pfizer as a controller. There are countless industry roles, and the responsibilities of these roles might vary significantly based on the industry. Even so, I am going to attempt to oversimplify and generalize what the more common roles are that might be viable options for those interested in the business side. You've got finance, strategy/operations, product management, sales, and marketing. Each of these is sure to encompass thousands of roles that I won't touch on here, and the positions are constantly evolving. Data has become a large part of any organization and so you will find roles like data analyst that could exist under any of these verticals. There will be roles in HR, general administration, and research and development as well.

I'm going to focus on what I see as the most typical and industry-agnostic opportunities, but to reiterate, this is far from exhaustive, and I recommend you investigate further across industries and companies if any of these broad categories are of particular interest to you. Compensation for industry roles will be extremely different from one to the next so even offering ranges feels potentially misleading. Take any of these estimates with a grain of salt and go check the jobs page at companies that might be a fit for you.

## Finance

Here, I'm referring to the finance division of any company. At the top of this organization is the CFO. That would be the highest level you could reach if you climbed the finance ranks. There are quite a few different finance roles that report up to the CFO.

The first one I'll discuss is financial planning and analysis (FP&A). FP&A handles forecasting, budgeting, and financial analysis. I worked in several different finance roles at Apple, so I'll use those as examples. FP&A at Apple forecasts unit sales, revenue, and cost across every product and region. It utilizes those forecasts to help guide management decisions and ensure that performance is on track to meet goals. There is a worldwide FP&A team that aggregates forecasts as well as regional FP&A teams that roll their numbers up to worldwide. FP&A adjacent corporate finance roles like sales finance would work with the sales teams to model the economics behind different deals or promotions, estimate how many incremental units would be sold at different price points, calculate metrics like the elasticity or cannibalization for various offers, help set sales quotas, and so on. They were responsible for any analytics that would help serve the sales team. Other corporate finance groups like real-estate finance would model out the financials of opening a new retail store, analyze individual store performance to advise on where improvements could be made, and report key performance indicators (KPIs) on behalf of the fleet. Just about every function of an organization including sales, real estate, operations, product marketing, and so on will have finance counterparts that advise on tasks like cost–benefit analysis, forecasting, or budgeting for those particular activities. Some roles will be more reporting centric while others will have more of a strategy component. The roles are likely to be quite cadenced with weekly, monthly, or quarterly meetings and deliverables. The work will likely be busiest around quarter close. Some folks enjoy becoming very familiar with the processes while others might find them repetitive.

These types of financial analyst roles are available right out of undergrad. Just how competitive they are is likely to depend on the prestige of the company though they will almost never be as competitive at the entry level as roles in consulting or finance. Hours will probably be quite reasonable, maybe around 50 per week with no weekend work and great job security. In big tech, the all-in compensation is likely to start shy of $100k with modest 10 percent or so raises year over year. At the middle management level, pay might be closer to $200k. While jobs like consulting are very much up or out, these FP&A roles are not. Whether or not you get promoted often depends on your direct manager either leaving or being promoted. As such, the trajectory can be much flatter and folks can more easily get stuck on the ladder, though they can also accelerate through it if they're a top performer. There are a few roles at the highest levels that everyone in the finance org competes for. One such position would be the head of FP&A of a global business where compensation will be very dependent on the size of the P&L, ranging anywhere from a few hundred thousand all the way up toward seven figures in rare cases. Regardless, FP&A can serve as a great route to CFO. If you do defy the odds and make it to CFO or finance head of a division at a large company, then the pay may be a couple million and there will be a significant amount of equity involved.

FP&A can be a great exit from just about anywhere in finance. On the flip side, exits from FP&A can feel limited. Some may try to push into more of a strategy role at their company or jump laterally to another finance role at a different company or perhaps a start-up. Others might be able to do it backward and battle their way into consulting as a lateral hire but exiting into the finance world will prove quite difficult. This is the position I found myself in and it's a large part of why I went to do my MBA. The MBA route is a good option for those hoping to pivot out of industry finance.

Another role within industry finance is corporate development. This is basically mergers and acquisitions (M&A). Companies like Apple have effectively brought the role of the M&A investment banker in-house. They have a group of ex-bankers that help carry out acquisitions and, if needed, might also do divestitures or partnerships. The role will be much like an M&A role at a bank. While some companies might accept analysts or lateral moves into the corp dev group, by and large, the most common way in will be after a stint in M&A investment banking. The hours are more similar to those of an FP&A analyst than a banker, think around 50 to 60 with variability based on active deals, but the pay, relative to banking, is substantially lower. The salary may be about the same but the bonus will be a fraction of what you'd earn at a bank. If you reach the head of corp dev level at a larger company, you could stand to make between $500k and $1M. Corp dev is seen as an exit, although one could potentially go back to banking later on or move to a different company. This role may not be on a CFO track since the scope of work is more niche than that of someone like an FP&A manager who sees the whole business, though this will depend on the company.

One more role within industry finance is treasury. These people manage a company's cash. They deal with investing it, managing debt load, raising capital, doing dividends or buybacks, and so on. Treasurers are generally not hired out of undergrad but instead have some experience in capital markets or investment management. The hours should be comparable to those of an FP&A role and the pay will likely be slightly better. At the head of treasury level, you would likely have the second highest-paying finance role after the CFO, anywhere from several hundred thousand up into seven figures at a large F500, though your pay, as always, would depend on a variety of factors. Treasury is also seen as an exit, so your natural options after being a treasurer might be switching to a different industry finance role, fighting for a CFO role, managing money for a fund, or moving laterally to the treasury team at a different company.

Finance roles are many and varied depending on the company in question so I'm not pretending to be exhaustive here. In the accounting section, I mentioned the industry accounting and controller path. There's also investor relations which deal with press releases, earnings announcement materials, dialogue with investors, and so on and could be a viable exit for folks with some sort of financial background. There may be other roles focused on risk or compliance as well. For the sake of brevity, I'll leave it there, but if the industry finance route is of interest to you, I'd recommend exploring roles within a particular company or industry and learning for yourself what those jobs entail. Larger companies, particularly big tech, are likely to have more roles and higher pay ceilings. They'll also have stronger brand names that might bolster your resume, especially early on in your career. That said, start-ups will also offer these types of roles and, if the company is successful and grows substantially while you're there, you might see your equity more than compensate for the smaller salary. Or not, that's the risk.

Industry roles tend to be very stable and, at the higher levels, can pay quite well. That said, reaching those high levels at big firms to achieve the kinds of seven-figure pay packages that I just mentioned is extremely difficult and frankly unlikely. If you want to keep doors open and optimize for exit opportunities, then you are likely better off starting in something like banking or consulting. You can always jump from one of those into industry, whereas moving from industry into one of those may prove quite difficult. But, if you know you want to be in a certain space or at a certain company, going straight in can make a lot of sense.

Rotational programs like the Finance Development Program at Apple have become popular for new grads and will give you the chance to try a variety of finance roles before choosing which one to permanently join. If you go the industry finance path right out of college, I'd recommend a rotational program like that. Otherwise, you may not know exactly what the role that you're signing up for entails. The more interesting roles tend to be less reporting focused, more revenue focused (meaning less cost/budgeting work), and have more of a strategy element to them. Consider those factors when reading through the job descriptions.

### A Conversation With a Former Financial Analyst

**What do you love about corporate finance, and are there some unexpected benefits you found the role to have that might not be advertised?**

*I loved that the role was structured, but still built upon itself each week and allowed for creativity and innovation. An unexpected benefit was that your workload was highly predictable. In my particular role (sales forecasting), I had crazy hours Monday through Wednesday, but things tapered off by Thursday or Friday and I never worked a weekend.*

*I liked that we were always solving a problem and it never felt competitive. We were all working toward the same goal and helping each other get there.*

**Speaking honestly, what did you hate about the role? Do you have any regrets taking the role and why?**

*I didn't like that I felt so busy all week, but when I stepped away from the role, I wasn't learning anything about the macro world like new industries and global events. I felt very siloed. No regrets at all—a great first job. I was learning a ton about how a company operates, how to work with a team, how* to build financial models, and so on. I just knew that long term, I would want to find a career path that challenges me to learn more about the world. However, I do somewhat regret not just doing investment banking to open more doors. Corporate finance doesn't help you pivot to that many roles, especially the older you get.

### What is the career growth potential like in the role?

Fast! There were many opportunities for management as a young person. I had an intern after less than one year on the job. My manager was less than 30 years old and managing a huge team.

Candidly—I don't think compensation growth potential was that high if you weren't lucky enough to get on an accelerated manager path. After reaching a certain level around three years in, I would have felt stagnated if not able to become a manager—especially since I did not get candid feedback around promotion timelines.

As mentioned above, it's a bit harder to pivot into other finance roles without an investment banking or consulting background.

### What advice do you have for someone hoping to follow in your footsteps?

Talk to as many people as you can about their jobs. Ask them about their day-to-day and their career aspirations. Find a mentor in college that you can discuss career paths with. It's easy to find a mentor once you have a job, but I always wished I had someone outside of my company to talk openly to.

Be open with your manager about compensation/getting promoted. At my company, if you aren't vocal about it, you won't get it.

In terms of recruiting for finance roles like mine, be able to answer two questions. One, why do you want to work at company X? And two, why do you want to do finance at company X? At least in my interview process, they really cared about number two, to weed out people applying for a finance job just to get a foot in the door.

The interviews are pretty behavioral. Technical questions will not be typical accounting, but rather how a business operates. Like how would you analyze the expansion of sales into a new market? How would you forecast a product that's the first of its kind? More about business frameworks, less about memorizing formulas.

**What did you see as your most viable exit opportunities?**

*Corporate finance or an operating role at another tech company. You can really sell yourself into anything if you're still young. Finance is highly cross-functional, so that's what I used as my selling point. Anything partnerships or business development is an easy path. Or, you could pivot into whatever function was adjacent to your finance role, like if you were in operations finance, you could work in an operations role like supply chain planning.*

# Strategy/Operations

Some roles are strategy, some are ops, some are both. Drawing a rigid dichotomy between the two would be misleading as most roles will include parts of each. Still, I'll first try to explain what strategy and operations represent, separately.

Think of strategy as internal consulting. You're basically doing the work that management consultants would do, but in-house. If your company is launching a new product, trying to grow sales, expanding geographically, introducing new initiatives, and so on, then the strategy team may have a hand in it. These would be the corporate strategy questions that determine the high-level direction of the firm. You might be doing market research, modeling, or even project management. Often, these roles require a lot of working cross-functionally with teams like finance, product, marketing, and sales. You may be project based or focused on a specific part of the business. In the project-based role, you will be part of a centralized team that works on projects across the business for a few weeks to a few months at a time. If your role is focused on one part of the business, you may have many ongoing work streams and will build a deep knowledge in one area.

To contrast, ops roles are more hands-on in terms of managing the value chain and the opportunities will vary depending on the business. Responsibilities could include reducing lead times, eliminating bottlenecks, improving capacity, implementing new tools, overseeing a budget, coordinating logistics, improving quality control processes, negotiating with suppliers, consolidating vendors, and selecting sites. The possibilities are endless. It's a very hands-on role and is much closer than other roles mentioned to quite literally running the business. There may be some travel to coordinate with suppliers, manufacturing, warehousing, or distribution so site visits may be a larger part of the job than would be the case for a finance role. It can be viewed as slightly less sexy than strategy and the work can sometimes be more repetitive and monotonous. Still, Tim Cook joined Apple in a supply chain role and ended up as CEO so there are certainly opportunities to climb the corporate ranks out of ops. It's an integral part of any business.

Strategy roles will generally have "strategic" or "strategy" in the job title whereas ops roles might be called "biz ops," "supply chain strategy," "operations management," and so on. "S&O" or "strat ops" would be roles that refer to some intersection of the two. Regardless of the name, it's likely that the roles will involve elements of both. One way to think of the relationship between strategy and ops is that there is a high-level corporate strategy that defines the overall direction of the firm, and there are the operations which have more to do with the implementation of that direction. These two groups may have significant overlap in some companies and be much more differentiated in others.

Strategy or strat ops roles may not pay as well as consulting but the hours and stability will be much better. In big tech, you're likely to work 45 to 60 hours per week and make somewhere around $100k at the entry level (though not all firms will have entry-level strat ops roles), $140k to $200k around the associate or manager level, and a few hundred thousand higher up. Chief operating officer (COO) or CEO would be the roles to aspire to where you could reach executive-level compensation. Roles that skew more heavily toward ops may earn a bit less across the board. If folks choose to leave strategy or strat ops, likely pivots include a business development role (more sales oriented), a chief of staff role (supporting the executive team across many of their responsibilities), or a jump to another tangential org like finance.

These strat ops roles can sometimes be available to new grads but generally hire people with experience. The typical background might be a business-related bachelor's degree along with any kind of work experience in consulting, banking, project management, business analytics, finance, or, of course, operations. Getting an MBA is another way in. The work tends to be a bit more interesting than what a comparable finance or sales role might offer so MBAs and consultants often shoot for strat ops. The more ops heavy and supply chain focused the role is, the more likely candidates will have technical operations experience or training rather than something like a general consulting background.

If you are interested in this space, I would still generally recommend doing consulting first. It will expose you to more industries, do a better job teaching you the strategy toolkit, surround you with the best and brightest, give you a strong first brand on your resume, pay you more, and keep more doors open for you. If you then decide you'd like to cut back on hours and travel and focus on the long-term strategy of a company rather than short advisory projects, internal strategy can offer some really great opportunities with comparable pay. You might be able to come in as an experienced hire often at a level more senior to what you would have achieved had you started your career at that company.

## A Conversation With a Google Employee Working in Strategy/Ops

**What do you love about corporate strategy/ops, and are there some unexpected benefits you've found the role to have that might not be advertised?**

*I love the flexibility to work on different projects and get to know all distinct subject matter while in the same role! You truly get to own things end to end, see through your recommendations, and work with high-level leadership to land key projects.*

**Speaking honestly, what do you hate about the role? Do you have any regrets taking the role and why?**

*I do not regret taking this role and genuinely love my job! However, when you work at a large company, there can be a lot of layers in decision making and bureaucracy to work through when making large decisions. You might need to go to eight orgs to make one decision. We'll need to make this one change, but we don't own anything that needs to change so I'm often herding cats.*

*Some teams separate strategy and ops where strategy is more sexy while ops tends to be more repetitive, like setting team goals, reporting, and doing the audit.*

**What is the career growth potential like in the role?**

*I think there's huge career potential in a strategy and operations org. You are positioned in the decision-making body of a company, which drives impact and solutions for both your customers and your workforce. The problems that you are solving in this role can be things that make or break a company of a smaller size.*

*They try to do a lot of shuffling between strategy and ops teams to keep people in the org but manager roles can be really restricted because they don't want to bloat at the middle management level. It would probably be easier to know more confidently about promotions at a smaller company. Compensation increases every year and there's an equity refresh every year. It's very formulaic at Google. The lowest-level executives, directors, probably make a million a year in mostly equity.*

**What advice do you have for someone hoping to follow in your footsteps?**

*One of the biggest advantages to going into an S&O role is being able to use data in decision making, collaborate effectively across organizations, be structured in problem-solving ambiguous questions, and thinking holistically about your solutions.*

*To get a sense of the roles, I would ask hiring managers if they're launching new initiatives, which would lean more strategy, or doing more quarterly stuff which tends to lean more toward ops.*

**What do you see as your most viable exit opportunities?**

*The skills you learn in S&O roles can be transferred to most other S&O orgs. You are well poised to take a leadership position at a smaller, more nimble company or go into biz ops at another company.*

*People might leave to start their own companies or to lead a function at a company that's not necessarily strat ops so that they can skip over being just a worker bee. You could be the head of sales, marketing, or finance. It would be rare to go back to consulting. You use data to drive decisions like everyone in the world so that skill set is broadly applicable. On the flip side, you can pretty much always switch into strat ops from something else.*

# Product Management

Think of the product manager (PM) as the CEO of a product. This role intricately coordinates with engineering, marketing, finance, UX (user experience), insights, and sales to ensure the success of the product. PMs play a pivotal role in shaping the strategies of various teams within a company, actively contributing to the evolution of ideas. As a result, they are not just spectators but rather active participants in the journey of turning a concept drawn on a whiteboard into a tangible reality.

The PM is responsible for creating and maintaining a product roadmap, in some cases several, and owning a clear vision for the product's direction. They conduct qualitative and quantitative market research and customer feedback, collaborate with UX designers to improve the product's look and feel, partner with marketing on go to market strategy, closely analyze performance data, and influence finance decisions within a company.

It's important to remember that a PM at one company may look quite different from a PM at another company. For example, a PM at a big tech company like Google may be confined to a very specific product while a PM at a start-up may be able to manage several products with several engineering teams and report directly into the C-suite. When pursuing a PM role, one should closely consider the company profile including industry, size (big tech versus start-up), mission, and potential growth opportunities.

The role has experienced a surge in popularity, with certain companies even creating positions specifically tailored for recent graduates. Irrespective of one's background, securing a PM offer is guaranteed to be competitive. It's a unique position that allows business-minded individuals to work directly on product(s).

A PM position is a lucrative career path, even outearning software engineers. In big tech companies like Google, entry-level pay can range from $150k to $200k. Over time, with around 6 to 9 years of experience, this can reach over $300k, before equity. In some cases, PMs at the VP level could make a million. Technical PMs (TPMs), a PM who is responsible for bridging the gap between technical teams, complex technical concepts, and business objectives, usually make $25K to $50K more than

PMs. Outside of large tech companies, pay can be lower and, of course, depends on your previous experience and market demand. While structured, the workload is demanding, with around 45 to 60 hours of work per week (dependent on company too).

PMs come from various backgrounds and some, if not most, randomly find their way into the role. Regardless, business experience helps with understanding data and market dynamics, while coding or user experience knowledge is useful for working with high-caliber engineers. MBAs, engineering, consulting, banking, and diverse experiences can make someone a strong PM candidate. Keep in mind that a PM regularly "manages" or oversees engineers and various business stakeholders, even when they are not directly under the PM's management; the ability to lead with influence is a key PM skill. A PM generally thrives on structure while remaining flexible and open minded as business objectives change. If you're able to show some kind of experience with all the above, even better. There is no one path.

PMs can explore different avenues later on, like moving to a PM role in another company, becoming VP of product management or vertical lead, launching their own product, moving into a tangential ops or strategy role, or, in rare cases, moving into VC.

It's a very unique job. PMs gain a lot of exposure to various business units, an opportunity that is rare in business. It's maybe the only structured role that allows business folks to directly create, build, and manage a product.

If you're someone who loves technology and product design from a business perspective, a career in product management could be a great option for you.

### A Conversation With a Former Product Manager

**What do you love about product management, and are there some unexpected benefits you've found the role to have that might not be advertised?**

*I love the fact that I get to work with all types of people—you're the bridge between every function (engineering, design, QA, and customers). Part of working with different roles is that you get to hear and work with different thoughts and perspectives. I've become a better listener since I started in* product, and it's helped me put myself in other people's shoes before making a decision or reacting to something. You also learn how to influence without authority—as a new PM, you'll rarely "manage" others but you'll always be the go-to person for a decision involving your product.

### Speaking honestly, what do you hate about the role? Do you have any regrets taking the role and why?

Product is a very ambiguous role—there's no right or wrong way to do it, and everyone does it slightly differently. You have to learn to do it your own way by acting as a sponge and observing and learning from others in the beginning. This is probably the most challenging part for me—it takes a while to get in a good rhythm, while simultaneously trying to gain credibility from team members. I have no regrets taking the role—once you find your own rhythm and way of doing things, it's the best outlet to be creative and to be the voice of the customer.

### What is the career growth potential like in the role?

It varies, but the typical growth curve goes as follows: associate PM → PM → Senior PM → principal PM → director PM → VP of product → chief product officer. Some companies, usually bigger companies, offer an Associate Product Manager (APM) role, typically for those with no product experience or for new graduates. Expect to be in this role for around two years. Smaller companies/start-ups may not have an APM role. You may continue on either a managerial route or an individual contributor (IC) path. If you want to stay as an IC, your growth potential may be capped after principal. Note that not all these roles are offered at every company; titles are very fluid in the product world and can depend on the type and size of company. For example, a principal PM at a big tech company may jump to a Series C start-up as their VP of product.

### What advice do you have for someone hoping to follow in your footsteps?

Try to stand out from the crowd! Product is a very popular role today, so it's that much more imperative to know (1) why product management, (2) why you would make a great PM (what about your experience and personality would make you excel at the job), and (3) why you're passionate about the company. Some practical ways to stand out are to pick a product you like, *interview a few people, create a focus group (can be friends), identify common pain points, think of a potential solution, and throw it all in a PowerPoint/wireframe. This is something you can add to your resume and can talk about during interviews/cold reach-outs.*

### What do you see as your most viable exit opportunities?

*Product: If you want to stay in the PM operator path, you can make your way up to director/VP/CPO.*

*Entrepreneurship: Starting your own company/joining a small start-up.*

*Venture capital: If you want to transition into an investor path, venture capital is becoming a popular exit opportunity as well.*

## Sales

The archetypical B2B (business-to-business) sales path would be to start at the entry level as an sales development representative (SDR) where you'll spend your time cold-calling and e-mailing to create leads. The all-in pay here is likely to be somewhere around $70k at a tech firm in a major city and the hours might fall between 40 and 50 per week. Tech tends to be an attractive industry for those hoping to start a career in sales as it offers great flexibility, opportunity, and pay relative to other industries. Software sales will typically pay a bit more than hardware sales.

After 18 to 24 months, SDRs would advance to the account executive level. These are the folks who manage SDRs, take the leads that they generate, and follow through on them to close deals. They are likely to have quotas and so pay will become more variable based on their numbers. Account execs might make around $160k in total compensation or on-target earnings (OTR).

After maybe five years of experience, you might be presented with two options. One would be to continue managing accounts but at increasingly larger scale. The other would be a sales manager position. In the sales manager role, you're likely to manage broader sales strategy, set quotas, and be held accountable for the sales numbers that roll up to you. In big tech where the pay is generally higher than most industries, sales managers might break $300k. If you are able to climb beyond that at a large company and reach a VP-equivalent level where you're responsible for a large business, the pay can touch seven figures.

On the downside, you may be held to difficult targets and have to cope with lots of rejection. Sales jobs may not be particularly secure if targets are not met and the job can become quite stressful.

On the flipside, sales roles are great for those who want to eat what they kill. Your compensation will be largely based on your performance and at the higher levels, the role can be quite lucrative with uncapped commission. The job has perhaps the best work–life balance of all the roles I've mentioned with lots of flexibility and very reasonable hours. You'll spend a lot of time working with people and attending events rather than just sitting at your computer, and the educational requirements to get into sales don't tend to be that high.

Most folks who go into sales are likely to remain in sales or maybe jump over to business development, partnerships, marketing, or customer success. Business development is similar to sales but with incentives tied less to pure sales numbers and more to certain initiatives or strategic objectives. Customer success is a role that on-boards new customers to the product, helps them with ongoing education and support, tries to eliminate churn, and serves as a partner in helping them get the most out of the product.

Sales might be a great fit if you enjoy working with people and earning commission-based pay while also being able to tolerate both rejection and the stress of having to hit targets.

### A Conversation With a Senior Account Executive at LinkedIn

**What do you love about sales and are there some unexpected benefits you've found the role to have that might not be advertised?**
*I love a lot of things about sales. Primarily, I enjoy engaging with people on a daily basis, having conversations, and building meaningful relationships. I love that as a salesperson, I am directly responsible for increasing the value of the company by growing revenue, stealing market share, and being more competitive overall.*

*I'm not quite sure there is a job that has a better work–life balance. I set my own calendar, apart from required internal meetings, and am able to more or less work from anywhere in the world. Beyond this, I am intensely competitive and want to be the best rep in our business. Sales is a fantastic outlet for this. I am driven by uncapped earnings and am certainly money motivated. Knowing that I have no limit to what I can earn in a fiscal year fuels me and forces me to work at my best.*

*When I first started my career, I didn't quite realize how strong some of the relationships I built would be and how meaningful they could be to me long term. I have connections at so many different companies, friends from incredibly diverse backgrounds, and should I ever want to pivot, there is no shortage of people in my network that I could leverage to make that happen.*

### Speaking honestly, what do you hate about the role? Do you have any regrets taking the role and why?

*I don't hate anything about my job or being in sales. What is incredibly challenging and can cause elevated periods of stress is having a quota. Being tied to a quota can cause stress in your day-to-day life if you don't manage your time properly and don't have a clear plan for how you are going to succeed. Additionally, quotas are typically set at the start of the year with many companies operating off of a yearly quota (some will do biannual quotas, and some set them every quarter, but the latter is rare). This can be incredibly frustrating for reps because if the macro environment trends negatively, your quota could very quickly become incredibly difficult to hit. Additionally, there is certainly a degree of luck involved in sales. If you are at a strong company that produces a high number of "inbound leads," then it's quite literally based on luck as to what kind of deal you might be presented with. For example, if you are a new business rep ("account executive"), one rep might take an inbound meeting where a potential customer is ready to sign a 10k contract whereas a rep on the same team could get an inbound meeting for a company ready to spend 500k. These sorts of instances are out of your control and can be frustrating and this is a part of being in sales. I have no regrets choosing sales as my career and plan to stay in sales, but it absolutely is not for everyone.*

### What is the career growth potential like in the role?

*Career growth potential is what excites me the most about being in sales. The promotion cycles are typically quicker than other jobs and, depending on what you want to do long term, it's typically somewhat easy to identify a path for how to get there early in your career. For example, I want to be a VP of sales. Right now, as a senior account executive, I'm gaining leadership experience by working with my SDRs and mentoring junior reps. From here, I plan to become an enterprise account director. Following that role, I would enter our large enterprise market as a senior account director. At this point, after several years as an individual contributor, I could make a really strong pivot into management where, again, I would plan my growth toward a VP role by going from sales manager to director to senior director before preparing for a VP position. It's very possible that I take this exact growth path. It's also possible I change my mind and want to do something else within sales, but regardless of what that is, the growth is there. Of course, you need to be at a company with growth potential in order to advance, but if you are excelling in your role as a salesperson, you will be continuously presented with opportunities to grow and sell more complex deals, work with larger customers, and make more money along the way.*

### What advice do you have for someone hoping to follow in your footsteps?

*Make yourself uncomfortable early. Understand that in sales you will get rejected consistently. Embrace this early in your career and you will take comfort in knowing that you are okay with being turned away and will focus more on improvement versus rejection. This will make it much easier to succeed in the future. Be curious now. Ask good questions in class, with your friends, and with strangers. Be a sponge.*

*When interviewing for a sales role, you should feel confident evaluating the manager just as much as they are evaluating you. Having a good manager is always important but it is absolutely critical in the first couple of roles you have. Evaluate for a few things. Are they genuinely a good person? Will they take the time to truly develop you? Is the company as a whole going to be invested in your growth as a salesperson? What kind of training does the manager have planned for you? What would success look like 6 to 12 months into the role? What is your growth potential there? A good manager will be excited to discuss all these things with you and will have a plan for them that is specific to your goals as a professional.*

**What do you see as your most viable exit opportunities?**

*I plan to be in sales my whole career—but I think something that is of interest, depending on how far into your sales career you go, would be to go into sales consulting. After being in leadership, I could see myself getting to a point where I might want to consult early-stage companies that are building out their sales orgs.*

# Marketing

A career in marketing could mean a lot of things depending on your interests and your skill set. There's internal marketing and there are agencies. The work could be creative or could be analytical. It has a less-defined path than many of the other roles I've mentioned. It will look different across industries and is constantly evolving. One important differentiation within roles is the extent to which jobs are creative or analytical. Though many people tend to see marketing as designing fun ads or coming up with catchy slogans, many of these creative jobs are outsourced to agencies. Those roles might have more to do with design, creating content, managing a social presence, and so on. Recruiters for those roles might expect to see a portfolio or some relevant examples to showcase experience. By and large, those are not the kinds of roles that I'm referring to here as those would go to more creative types. Instead, I'm focusing on roles that would appeal to folks interested in the business side of marketing. While internal roles do have some creative components, the day-to-day responsibilities primarily entail building, maintaining, and optimizing the effectiveness of different marketing channels. Duties might involve market research, price setting, capital allocation, conversion rate analytics, retention, and so on. To go a little deeper, let's break internal marketing down into some of the more common roles that you might find at large companies.

Product marketing is in charge of the entire funnel from awareness and consideration to conversion and retention for certain products. Product marketing tends to be very analytical, optimizing KPIs across campaigns and channels, running A/B tests to see what works, conducting studies with customers, tweaking product features or prices, and so on. It is strategic in terms of evaluating the market, developing the right messaging and positioning of the product, and developing the right go-to market strategy. All of this makes it a particularly good fit for ex-consultants or MBA grads.

Demand generation will focus more on the top of the funnel. It's all about generating leads and building awareness across marketing channels. Channels include social media, e-mail, search, and traditional. Demand generation will think about how to reach certain customer segments and pull the right levers to build loyalty.

Brand marketing also focuses specifically on building awareness. Brand marketing will help run campaigns to drive traffic and may think more about the brand as a whole rather than just specific products. Brand marketing takes a long-term view of building the value of the business and ensuring that the brand is presented in an effective and cohesive way.

There are also channel marketing roles that focus on one channel, creative marketing roles that do the creative work in-house rather than outsourcing it to agencies, and many other marketing roles that go by slightly different names. At the end of the day, all have to do with building a brand and promoting it effectively.

There are some roles available directly out of undergrad, but it usually takes one to two years of general experience before switching into marketing. For roles available directly out of undergrad, many will be "just-in-time" hiring. This means that you'll see openings pop up during the spring semester of your senior year. Some larger companies may have more robust marketing programs that accept applications in the fall, but those are less common. Some role titles available to undergrads might be marketing specialist, marketing associate, marketing assistant, or marketing coordinator. The more common path would be to start in a different department and then transition into marketing after a couple of years. Folks who take this track might start in sales, communications, product, analytics, public relations (PR), or social media. If you do start in one of these departments, there may not be a structured path into marketing, so making the switch might require some hustle. Others will have more structured internal mobility pathways.

The marketing lifestyle is known to be quite good with very reasonable hours, though the pay scale tends to start low and rises exponentially as you advance through your career. For internal roles, pay is likely to be between $50k and $80k at the entry level and could reach around $200k to $300k after a decade or so. There is huge variability here depending on the company and the role. Chief marketing officer would be the top of the food chain here though possible pivots might include a jump to tangential functions at the same company, namely sales or public relations, a move into a different functional area within marketing, or a similar role at a different company.

A marketing career offers the opportunity to be creative, strategic, and influential in promoting products or services. You get to analyze market trends, target audiences, and develop campaigns to connect with customers. It's a field with diverse roles, potential for advancement, and the chance to make a significant impact on a company's success.

This is a great option for those who want a more creative tilt to their career with great hours, solid earning potential, and variability in daily responsibilities.

### A Conversation With a Product Marketing Manager at LinkedIn

**What do you love about marketing and are there some unexpected benefits you've found the role to have that might not be advertised?**
*The biggest unexpected benefit of working in marketing is the sheer exposure you get to the rest of the business. Regardless of what function you might be in within marketing (i.e., demand generation, product marketing, brand marketing, etc.), there is very much an interdisciplinary approach that allows you to understand how sales, product management, legal, and operations need to come together to successfully run a business. This is particularly helpful if you have ambitions to be either a COO or CMO.*

*At the end of the day, to be successful in your role, you must be able to work cross-functionally, and, by doing so, you're constantly learning about other people's roles and what they need to be effective.*

**Speaking honestly, what do you hate about the role? Do you have any regrets taking the role or going into marketing and why?**
*While I don't have any regrets about taking a role in marketing, the biggest pain point is there are times where it can be heavily operational and project*

*management oriented. Meticulous organization is not a skill that comes naturally to me, and the more senior I get, the more important it becomes. The reason this is so important is because marketing tends to be the glue between different functions, so you're also on the hook for making sure cross-functional partners are on the hook to deliver their projects for a go-to market to be successful. Second, measuring your impact as a marketer can be quite ambiguous depending on the role that you pick, and this can be frustrating when trying to make a case for promotions. This is specifically true of roles that are not closely connected to revenue (i.e., product marketing or content marketing), where there is room for a lot more subjectivity when it comes to performance evaluation, especially since different people's projects can vary widely.*

**What is the career growth potential like in the role?**

*Generally, there are a lot of different growth paths you could take in marketing. Depending on which function you choose within marketing, you're likely to find yourself in a specialist or a generalist capacity. For example, working in consumer acquisition or paid media would very much lead you to being an ads specialist; however, working in product marketing lends itself to being a research expert but also having a general understanding of how the business works.*

**What advice do you have for someone hoping to follow in your footsteps?**

*If you're generally a curious person, then try it. There is a lot of variety in the world of marketing and it's very rare that there isn't something for everyone. At a minimum, it's a gateway career to another role that might end up being more interesting, but I have never felt that there was a shortage of options by working in marketing.*

**What do you see as your most viable exit opportunities?**

*This very much depends on the role within marketing. Product marketing could pivot into pretty much any function and potentially even product management. Brand marketing or demand generation could also look at sales.*

# CHAPTER 6

# MBA

An MBA can be a great way to improve your career outlook or facilitate a pivot. It is the most common, most valuable, and most widely applicable graduate degree for those interested in working in business. That said, it is often not needed. I did my MBA at Columbia Business School and want to share what an MBA entails and what the purpose is.

An MBA or Master of Business Administration is a two-year degree that most folks do after they have at least two years of work experience. Applicants might range from 25 at the low end to 35 at the high end, though there are no actual age requirements.

There are several reasons to get an MBA. One is to make a pivot. Whether or not you have a background in a business-related field, an MBA will help bolster your resume and give you the chance to learn new skills, network with folks who have similar interests, access the alumni network to track down the right contacts, and dedicate yourself toward finding and securing the right role, often through much more structured pipelines than you would find off-cycle. I know people who were teachers before and wanted to become bankers, engineers before who wanted to become venture capitalists, and bankers who wanted to move into private equity. The list of career changers is long and varied.

I worked in an industry FP&A role and wanted to switch to consulting. Before the MBA, I tried to network and cold e-mail my way in. I found that the firms I spoke to were not really looking to bring on experienced hires, at least not me and not then. One possibility a consulting recruiter mentioned to me was to wait for the undergrad recruiting process to start and then apply as part of that through my alma mater college. That would have meant gunning for an entry-level role after several years of work, which made me feel like my career up to that point had been a waste. It also would have been very difficult to figure out how to prepare, who to do mock case interviews with, and how to find the time, not to mention convincing the career management center at my old undergrad to let me apply through them. That's not to say it's impossible to get a role as an experienced hire, but, at that point in time, it certainly did not feel like a great option to me. Getting an MBA was my solution to all that. Once I got in, the management consulting club set us up with contacts at every firm, timelines for when everything happens, happy hours to meet consultants, coffee chats with recruiters, partners for casing, and so on. I suddenly had access to more case interview prep material than I could ever read and a hundred other students eager to practice, enabling me to do over 70 mock cases before interviews even started. I worked on hands-on nonprofit consulting projects in New York, Kenya, and Vietnam that helped teach me what it's like to be a consultant. I got to take strategy classes to learn more about how consultants approach problems. I got to befriend many ex- and future consultants who served as mentors, in a sense, along the way. I was able to do a summer internship to make sure that consulting was in fact for me, and I was able to build a large network of other consultants across firms, all of whom could be co-workers or relevant decision makers as my career progresses. None of that would have been possible without the MBA. For those with nonbusiness backgrounds, the curriculum may be particularly valuable, offering them the chance to learn the basics and be effectively certified for having learned them.

Another reason for an MBA is career advancement. You might look up the hierarchy at work and realize that many of your superiors have MBAs. They might expect you to get one if you want to keep climbing. Some firms will sponsor employees to get an MBA, that is, pay for it. Some folks in PE, for example, use it to enable them to get a job at a better PE shop. Some just vaguely believe that having the MBA on your resume will open doors down the line. It will certainly teach you a bit more about how to interview and build a resume, what other opportunities are out there, how to conduct yourself in a networking setting, and just generally smooth your edges.

Another reason is the network. This is one of the intangibles that can have big payoffs down the line. Anyone from the network that you build could end up being a future investor, someone who hires you, someone who you hire, someone who you sell work to, an intellectual partner, and so on. You never know where those people will end up, but many will likely be in the upper echelons of the business world.

Another reason is to start a business. While most people won't fall into this bucket, business school can serve as an incubator, giving you years to pursue an idea, professors to help, students to partner with, engineering school students to leverage, funding, a place to work, an alumni network full of contacts, and classes on entrepreneurship. I had classmates that launched a canned Sangria business during business school. They partnered with one another after meeting at school and hosted marketing parties for their classmates. It never would have happened had they not had those MBA years to pursue it. Even if you don't pursue entrepreneurship during your two years, you're likely to leave feeling much more prepared to start a business down the line.

Another reason to get an MBA is for the fun of it. It's two years in a new place full of happy hours, travel, new friends, and school breaks, all in the name of doing something productive for your career. Part of the calculus for me doing an MBA was that I felt complacent and a bit bored. I wanted to mix things up and really enjoy my 20s. An MBA gave me the chance to quit my job, move to Manhattan, double the number of friends I had, party like I was in college again, and travel to 17 countries between day one and graduation. It was an unbelievable two years and a break from work that I will never regret taking. With almost 50 percent of our class being international students, I met people from all around the world and got to broaden my global perspective quite a lot.

One more reason for an MBA is that it's an excellent dating service. I met my now girlfriend there. You spend two years having fun and getting to know a big group of people, all of whom are similarly ambitious and around your age. It's a great pool to choose from and business school couples are common.

On the flip side, there's the hefty price tag that comes out to around $250k once you account for housing, tuition, and expenses. There's also the opportunity cost of giving up two years of income and the fact that you aren't guaranteed a better job. You should really come in with an idea of what you want to get out of it so that you aren't leaving anything on the table or looking back wishing you'd done it differently. You only have one shot at it. Everybody's situation is unique and it's a big decision. If you know you want to go, you can be intentional about saving up money, applying for scholarships, getting student loans, or raising money some other way. While it can be very helpful to some, many employers may not see the value in it and some may view it as being historically more relevant than it is now.

In order to apply, you have to take either the GMAT or the GRE, which are standardized tests similar to the SAT. It's common to study a couple of hours per day for several months prior to taking the test and many people take it multiple times until they get a score they're happy with. Once taken, the score is valid for five years, regardless of which test you take. Most people will take the test after college while they are working, although some people even take it during college. The application process is much like applying to college, except that there is no common app. You'll have to write some essays that likely have to do with why you want to get an MBA and why you want to go to that particular school, and you'll need a couple of referrals from folks who are most likely managers you've had thus far in your career.

In your application, you'll want to highlight leadership qualities either through work or through extracurricular activities. Much like with under-grad applications, you want to tell a good story. I had played basketball in college and, after graduating from college, coached a youth basketball team. I was able to connect those experiences, paint basketball as a passion of mine, and give examples of how coaching made me a better leader. When I received my acceptance phone call from Columbia, I was told that they liked that part of my application. It was something unique to me and I believe it made me stand out. Finding creative ways to show things like passion, leadership, entrepreneurship, teamwork, work ethic, and so on in your application can help set you apart and, if you know that you will be applying to business school, you can intentionally put yourself in positions or roles that will make for good stories.

You don't need to know exactly what it is that you want to do after the MBA or with your career in general, but the more confident and intentional you can sound in your essays, the better off you'll be. I'd venture to say that maybe half of the people I spoke to about this didn't end up in the kind of job that their essays claimed they would.

It's generally seen that doing an MBA is only worth it if you attend a top 20 or so business school. The M7 are historically viewed as the top of the list with Stanford, Harvard, and Wharton as the three most prestigious. The other four of the M7 are Sloan, Columbia, Kellogg, and Booth. That said, M7 is just a construct and there are quite a few others of similar caliber.

Some schools offer 2+2 programs which you'd apply to during college, and the idea is that you would work for two years, though you can work more if desired, before starting your two-year MBA. This can help line up your five-year plan early on but I would only recommend going through with the MBA, when the time comes, if you know what you want to get out of it and believe that is the right time to do it. Otherwise, you risk spending a whole lot of money and not optimizing your Return on Investment (ROI).

During school, you can focus on whatever subjects you're interested in. Columbia has a value-investing program, a private equity program, and many more. If entrepreneurship is what you're interested in, then you can fill your schedule with classes focused on that. One big difference between undergrad and MBA is that, in college, the classes tend to be more run-of-the-mill introductory courses. In MBA, the classes can get pretty niche so you can really learn about whatever you want. For example, I took a class called "a strategic marketing approach to private equity in emerging markets."

Clubs are a big part of the MBA experience as they lead the charge on not just the professional activities but also the recreational ones. We had a wine club, a beer club, and a spirits club, all separate from one another. There are many opportunities to get real-world experience whether through classes, clubs, or internships. Columbia covered flight costs to send me and a group of friends to Nairobi, Kenya, to meet with a medical device start-up that we'd been consulting for throughout the semester. On that note, there are also many travel opportunities. The school hosted world tours which are like networking trips, immersion classes which are professor-led consulting projects that travel, and exchanges which are study abroad programs at other MBA schools. I did a brief exchange at the University of Cape Town in South Africa.

People often say that you will be so busy that you'll need to pick two of the three: social, professional, and academic. While there are certainly tradeoffs and your calendar is likely to be packed full of events, there's also no reason you can't juggle all three. Just how busy you are during your MBA is up to you. Classes are very difficult to fail so the amount of effort and time you put into them is really about how much you want to get out of them. The same goes for networking and recruiting. You build your own adventure.

Whether or not an MBA will be worth it for you depends on your career path. Many industries have post-MBA roles, many of which I've mentioned so far, and so further researching those roles could help you set goals and understand whether or not the ROI will make sense for you. If you're in a job that you like and you see a clear path upward, then you likely don't need the degree and, while you'd certainly enjoy your time there, you may not be able to justify it.

I would highly recommend you to take a look at the employment report of a business school like Harvard, Wharton, and Stanford. These reports are available online and published annually. I think they are a helpful reference point to see where some of the brightest business minds are ending up. While your options may be more limited than those of Wharton students or you may not be coming out of business school, it is always worth considering what smart people in a similar domain are doing. It's not a perfect science but, directionally, this can tell you a lot about which kinds of roles those folks see value in. These reports include salary information, names of hiring companies, and the split by both industry and function. Just about every MBA program publishes one annually.

If it's more school that you want, you could alternatively do a PhD and put yourself on the path to academia. You can get a PhD in all sorts of areas within finance, business, economics, math, and so on. These programs may take about five years and will generally pay an annual stipend between $20k and $50k depending on the school and the field. The work will be research intensive and you will also be helping teach classes along the way. PhDs are a hot commodity for some of the more technical roles I've touched on like hedge funds though the one "exit option" that is exclusive to PhDs is becoming a professor.

There are, of course, countless other postgraduate programs that might give you a leg up as well but, for the sake of brevity, I will leave it at that.

# CHAPTER 7

# Other Career Selection Criteria

Please recognize that this has not been exhaustive. I didn't touch on the role of an entrepreneur, a merchant at a clothing retailer, an actuary at an insurer, or countless other career paths. Consider this, instead, an introductory framework for how to navigate the various domains and an outline of the more typical career pipelines that appeal to ambitious people interested in business or finance. Take from it what you can and go on to do your own research in the areas that interest you or those that you believe I've left unexplored.

Choosing your first job is a big deal and you only get to do it once. While your career may not seem like a huge part of your life as you're growing up and going through school, I assure you it will be. Don't just stumble into that career; be intentional about it. Reach out to school alumni, friends' parents, career advisors, and professors. It will take hustle and preparation. Get creative. Whatever it takes.

Think about what's important to you. Where do you want to live? Where will your friends and family be? What do you envision doing in the long term? How important is money to you? How important is lifestyle to you? Do you want to work remote? Are you more quantitative or more creative? What are your realistic options? Are you willing to go back to school?

Build your application steadily. Recruiters will look at your GPA and some might even ask for your SAT scores. Take these things seriously. Be a well-rounded applicant. Find creative ways to show your interests outside of class. Find internships that set you up for the next internships. Word and structure your resume carefully.

Choose your industry. Some of the roles I mentioned won't require industry-specific choices up front. Others will. You may become an industry specialist, you may become a functional specialist, or you may become both. Regardless, you'll be working on one industry or another; so, what intrigues you? What are you passionate about? Industries likely won't pigeonhole you in the same way that your function might, so you'll likely have opportunities to reconfigure this decision as you go. There's technology, health care, consumer products, retail, financial services, telecom, manufacturing, energy, media and entertainment, travel and hospitality, nonprofit, real estate, consulting, legal, accounting, and so on. Think about what excites you. Think about what your values are. Think about what you would be good at. Use foresight. Think about which of these roles will more easily be supplanted by technology and automation. Think about which industries might fade and which are emerging. Climate or artificial intelligence would be examples of these more nascent and growing domains.

Consider where you are willing to move. Moreover, consider where you want to move. Your career can take you many places. Large companies may enable you to more easily relocate. Major cities are likely to offer the best opportunities. San Francisco is the heart of technology. New York is the heart of finance. Both are expensive to live in but may also offer higher pay to compensate for that. I believe in moving to a big city in your 20s to get your career started. You'll put yourself in the best position to learn and be promoted. You'll be surrounded by like-minded and ambitious people. You'll be exposed to what else is out there and motivated by the competitive drive and energy that the city emits. You've surely heard Frank Sinatra's lyrics about New York: "If I can make it there, I'll make it anywhere." You can always leave the big city, but the personal and professional growth that you'll get from starting a career there can be invaluable and will help you combat complacency. Working abroad can also be an exciting option. Countries like France or Australia are sure to offer compelling work–life balance alternatives to what you might find in the United States. That said, the pay in most countries will be at a substantial discount to what you'll find in the United States. For example, the salaries offered to post-MBA bankers in London versus New York can be ~40 percent lower. Some countries that do tend to offer compensation more on par with that of the United States are Switzerland, the UAE, and Singapore, though it, of course, depends on the role and the company. You'll also have to consider the language barrier. English will obviously be sufficient in Canada, Ireland, the United Kingdom, and Australia. It's also likely to be enough in the Nordics, parts of the Middle East, parts of Southeast Asia, South Africa, and selectively across parts of Europe. Generally, folks from around the world want to come to the United States, namely, one of the big cities, so starting your career in the United States will likely give you the most leverage to make whatever moves you want later on.

Think about what your dream job would be and then work backward. You want to build a cohesive roadmap for what your career might look like. If you have a sense of where you want to end up, then it will be much easier to figure out where you should start. Even so, you'll be constantly calibrating, and odds are you'll change your mind as you learn and as you go. It's normal nowadays to have several different careers over your lifetime. Be careful about closing doors that you aren't yet ready to forgo. Exit opportunities are hugely important early on in your career. Every career decision redesigns your universe of possibilities. Don't be afraid to take a step back in order to take a couple forward. Take risks. Think for the long term.

Jobs are constantly evolving and what I've laid forth is not exhaustive, so don't feel limited to it. If nothing so far excites you, look elsewhere. If you have a vision of a different kind of work, do the research and seek it out; the odds are that something like it exists. Think about which of these career paths might best match with the lifestyle you'd like to live and the legacy you'd like to leave. Think big and think now.

# CHAPTER 8

# Preparing for the Application Process

## Outreach

Outreach is mission critical. While it might be tempting to just submit your resume and leave it at that, reaching out to set up time with someone from the company will elevate your chances immeasurably. LinkedIn is a great place to start. If you can track down any fellow school alumni or first or second connections that work there, those might be your best shot. Your school likely has an alumni directory, so use that to track down contact information. If you can't find an e-mail there, you can try sending a message over LinkedIn. You can also try to guess their corporate e-mails. If I were trying to get in touch with someone at Uber, I might try john.smith@uber.com, jsmith@uber.com, johnsmith@uber.com, smith@uber.com, jonathan.smith@uber.com, and so on. E-mails are not case sensitive, so lower-case letters are fine. If your school or the company's website is able to provide the contact information of recruiters, then that would be another great approach. You could ask the recruiter to talk or if you can think of more specific on-the-job questions, you can ask the recruiter to put you in touch with someone that can help answer them. Ideally, you would do this outreach before submitting your application, but it can also be helpful even if you've already submitted. You can also try to leverage your personal network by letting it be known to your family and friends that you're interested in company X. This allows them to bring any contacts that they might have to your attention. Hustle is the name of the game.

When you reach out, keep the e-mail concise, introduce yourself, ask politely if they would be willing to take 15 or 30 minutes to chat with you and then propose some times that would work and let them choose.

Don't presume that they will say yes and keep your tone both humble and grateful. Here is an example of an outreach e-mail to a Tufts alumni working in finance at Apple:

Subject: Coffee Chat—Tufts Student

Hey Sara,

I'm a rising junior at Tufts and I'm really interested in the FDP internship program at Apple. I'm sure you're quite busy, but if you have 30 minutes to spare, I would love to chat and ask you some questions about your experience with the program. If you're up for it, just let me know what time works for you and I'll send over a Zoom invite. Here are some times that would work for me:

—Tuesday 3/14 from 2 p.m. to 6 p.m. PST

—Wednesday 3/15 from 9 a.m. to 12 p.m. PST

—Friday 3/17 from 1 p.m. to 5 p.m. PST

I'm also happy to propose times next week if none of these work. Looking forward to hearing back and thank you in advance!

Best,

John

——————————

Make sure you express the times in their time zone and don't forget to follow up with the Zoom invite. You'll want to make sure that you've done some baseline research before going into these conversations so that you can answer the question: What interests you about this role? You'll also want to have a quick, 30-second, "about me" pitch ready to go. When it comes time for you to ask them questions, you shouldn't ask ones that can be easily found online. Consider asking more open-ended questions like: How do you like the job? What have been your favorite parts of the role? What are the most difficult parts of the job? What has surprised you the most about the role? What is the team like? Is there anything you would have done differently if you were back in my position applying? What do you think has made you successful in the role? How are the opportunities for career growth? Have your managers been open to you trying new things or exploring other roles? Do you feel like you're still learning every day? What does a typical day look like for you? Where do most of your peers end up after two, three, four, and five years? What is the culture like in the office?

Ask questions that will be helpful to you, not just what you think they want to hear. At the same time, questions about pay, time off, exit opportunities, or hours can come off poorly, so tread carefully on these topics. Once time is up, be sure to say something like "I know we're coming up on time so I don't want to keep you any longer but I really appreciate you taking the time to talk with me." If they offer to introduce you to someone else or to help refer you, great, but I wouldn't ask for these things unprompted. After the call, you should always send a thank you e-mail. After that, you can try to keep in touch, but be wary of overdoing it. I would reach out only if you come across something that is relevant to the conversation you had that you think they might appreciate, if you have an important follow-up question, or if you want to let them know that you just submitted your application.

There is no harm in talking to a few people at the company you're interested in, but don't feel like you need to overdo it. It's about quality, so if you talk to one person and hit it off, then that may be plenty. On the calls, don't try to show off, don't be frantic, don't be weird, just be you. Make it a normal human-to-human conversation.

## Behavioral Interview

Interviews will always have a behavioral component. You will want to have stories prepared that can address "tell me about a time" questions. You'll want them to exemplify traits like problem solving, leadership, persuasion, perseverance, entrepreneurship, and teamwork. If your stories involve several of these, then they will be more versatile, and you can use them to answer more questions. Make sure that they're engaging. You want stories that would captivate, rather than bore, even a friend. Make them largely about people. If they're just about you performing a task, they are likely to bore your interviewer. I've witnessed countless smart people tell interview stories and the most common mistake they make is sounding robotic. They will drone on about data they worked with and some result they got, and I come away from it thinking wow, that was dull and meaningless to me. Be human. Be excitable, engaged, animated, and interesting! Be someone that the interviewer might want to hang out with. If it's a good interview, it should be a fun conversation.

Try timing yourself and practice delivering your stories in less than two minutes. Think STAR—situation, task, action, and result. You want to give brief context, touch on what you did, the results that you achieved, and also, ideally, the learnings that you took away from it. Here is an example of a story (I partially fabricated for illustrative purposes) that I believe delivers on the elements I just mentioned:

When I was on our geographic expansion team, we received a proposal for a brand-new store opening in Texas. It would be in a metro where we already had two stores, so this would be the third. The team was super excited about it as it would be in this up-and-coming mall. It was my job to make sure that it made financial sense. As I worked through the numbers, I started to question whether the market there was big enough to justify three stores. Knowing how excited the team was about this new location, I asked my manager if we would consider closing one of the existing ones. He was surprised. That wasn't part of the company's strategy at the time. We were expanding, not contracting. That said, he told me I was welcome to test it out if I had the bandwidth. So, I reverse-engineered our store opening model to fit what a store closure would look like. The result I arrived at was that it would, in fact, make sense to close one of the two current stores if we were opening a new one. So, my manager and I got this topic on the agenda at our next big meeting. I set up time with key stakeholders, like analytics and market development, to try and get their buy-in. I walked them through the numbers and was able to incorporate their feedback and build sensitivities around the assumptions that they were less confident about. Once we were largely aligned, it was time for the big meeting with all the retail leaders, including the CFO of retail. As I walked the group through our findings, I was surprised at how much push-back I got. These peoples' careers are built around the success of these stores and the growth of our fleet so to propose closing one seemed, to them, almost treacherous. But, I knew my numbers inside and out, I was calm, and I had buy-in from the important groups I'd met with beforehand. Ultimately, the heads of retail agreed, and we got approval to close the store, saving the company an estimated five million dollars. It was something you could read about in the news which was very cool to see. Store closures actually became a part of the real-estate strategy thereafter as we evaluated poor performers using the model I built and closed more stores throughout the pandemic. It was a really interesting lesson on the importance of working with, rather than against, cross-functional teams and also not being afraid to take chances and push forward new ideas.

The story could work for questions on persuasion, results, teamwork, entrepreneurship, challenges, and so on. I would just emphasize certain parts of the story more or less depending on the prompt. Most importantly, it's a story with people and problems rather than just a summary of a task. Notice that the result is quantified numerically. This makes the impact clear and the story more impressive.

Here's one more:

I was a volunteer youth basketball coach, and this one year at try-outs we had so many kids that the club decided to make an A team and a B team. That way, more kids would have a chance to participate. I offered to coach the B team. That meant the players were not as good, which, of course, presented a bit more of a challenge as a coach. So, I thought a lot about it and came up with a few strategies that I felt could help the team and the kids. I wanted to create a team where people were fearless, so I made sure not to pull kids out of the game when they made a mistake. That way, they wouldn't be afraid to take risks, play freely, and try things. I wanted to create a team where everyone was developing their basketball IQ, so rather than traditional X's and O's, I implemented a free-flowing offense where players had to make their own reads and decisions based on what the defense gave them. This forced them to think more carefully about every cut, screen, or pass that they made. I also wanted to encourage players to be invested in their own improvement. So, rather than lecture them after each game about what they needed to improve, I would create a dialogue and call on kids to give me their opinions of what went well and what didn't. That way, they would have to think and reflect rather than just listen, and they could hold themselves and each other accountable. Despite a really rocky start to the season, we actually won our last tournament of the year. Our B team saw much more camaraderie and growth than the A team, so much so that the A team coach asked me if I would coach the A team next year. Even though it was just working with kids, that experience taught me a lot about leadership and how to empower a team.

This one is not a work experience story, but it can still be effective, particularly if you're a student with limited experience. Stories like this can keep things fun and light while still being reflective and insightful. The types of stories you tell might also have to do with who your interviewer is and whether or not you think a given story will resonate with him or her.

Make sure you have enough stories ready to go as you may get multiple questions and multiple interviewers. You do not want to tell the same story twice. Also, as you practice, be sure to cut down on the excess. Notice which filler words you are using, such as "um," "like," or "sort of," and try to eliminate them. If there are certain sentences that are not absolutely necessary for the story, cut them out. You want to show that you are an effective communicator.

Beyond stories, you will want to be ready for other common behavioral interview questions. Here are some worth preparing for: What are your strengths? What are your weaknesses? What interests you about this role? Why are you applying to this company? Tell me about yourself. What is your 5-year or 10-year plan? What's the last book you read? What kind of news do you keep up with? Can you teach me something? Can you tell me a joke?

All of these are questions that I have gotten in interviews. I've even gotten riddles. You bring home 100 lbs of potatoes. They consist of

99 percent water. You leave them outside overnight and the next morning they consist of 98 percent water. What is their new weight?

For those of you taking the time to solve it, it's 50 lbs.

Just keep your cool and don't stress it. If you don't know something, you can just say that. The behavioral portion of interviewing is often overlooked, but it is extremely important so do not skip over the preparation.

## Resume

The resume is the cornerstone of any application so hopefully you're spending plenty of time perfecting yours. Any college will have resources to help work with you on your resume and ensure that it is in an acceptable format. I highly recommend taking advantage of those resources and working on yours with the career center. While I won't go too in-depth on resume building as it is a bit out of scope, I'll touch on just a few points.

There are a few important considerations when writing about your experiences. One is to show results. Wherever possible, include in your bullet points numbers to quantify what exactly you achieved. You also want to use strong verbs to explain your accomplishments. Consider terms like led, built, drove, constructed, identified, closed, structured, managed, or accomplished. Avoid terms like looked at, participated in, analyzed, helped, worked on, or attempted. These aren't hard-and-fast rules, but you want to show impact.

I would definitely include interests at the end of the page and have some fun stuff on that line that makes you stand out. It can lighten the mood and spark more enjoyable conversation. When I interviewed people, I always read that part to try and connect with the applicant on something. The interests on my resume include cliff jumping, Japanese food (90 restaurants in 90 days in Tokyo), and Warriors basketball. The first is unusual, the second is intriguing, and the third can spark banter if the interviewer cares about a team. Make them conversation starters. I would avoid including interests like movies, travel, reading, running, and cooking, unless you have a fun fact to accompany it. These will make you blend in and, frankly, come off as boring.

# CHAPTER 9

# Final Word

I hope you've found this helpful. My intent was to offer a good starting point and help elucidate what paths stand before you. Choosing what you want to be is a big decision and it can be scary. It's also exciting. While I want to instill just how important it is to make an informed first decision, I also don't want to discourage you if you feel that you did not or may not make the right choice. Hope is not lost. Just because I talk about specific exit opportunities, pay ranges, or the downsides to any role does not mean you are confined to those. You can create your own path and there will always be a way to get where you want if you're willing to put in the work. You'll notice from the interview portions at the end of each section that nobody I talked to truly hates or regrets taking their job. You may not make the perfect choice. You might just need to start working to figure out what you do and don't like. You can always calibrate from there. I don't know a single person that truly understood all their career options, made the perfect decision, and stuck with it indefinitely. They all just made a guess and then made the most of where they ended up. That's the norm. Still, I hope after reading this, you are a step ahead of that norm.

Whether you're in high school, college, or underway in your career, it's the right time to think deeply about the kind of career you want to have. Just start thinking about what you can do, one day at a time, to position yourself for whatever it is you want. It is attainable.

Best of luck.

# About the Author

**Joseph A. Malgesini** holds an MBA from Columbia Business School, an MA in finance from Claremont McKenna College, and a BA in economics and accounting. His background is in management consulting and big tech. He grew up in the San Francisco Bay area and now resides in New York City.

# Index

## OTHER TITLES IN THE BUSINESS CAREER DEVELOPMENT COLLECTION

Vilma Barr, Consultant, Editor

- *Make Your Internship Count* by Marti Fischer
- *Sales Excellence* by Eden White
- *How to Think Strategically* by Greg Githens
- *Succeeding as a Young Entrepreneur* by Harvey Morton
- *The Intentional Mindset* by Jane Frankel
- *Still Room for Humans* by Stan Schatt
- *Am I Doing This Right?* by Tony D. Thelen, Matthew C. Mitchell and Jeffrey A. Kappen
- *Telling Your Story, Building Your Brand* by Henry Wong
- *Social Media Is About People* by Cassandra Bailey and Dana M. Schmidt
- *Pay Attention!* by Cassandra M. Bailey and Dana M. Schmidt
- *Remaining Relevant* by Karen Lawson
- *The Road to Champagne* by Alejandro Colindres Frañó
- *Burn Ladders. Build Bridges* by Alan M. Patterson
- *Decoding Your STEM Career* by Peter J Devenyi

# Concise and Applied Business Books

The Collection listed above is one of 30 business subject collections that Business Expert Press has grown to make BEP a premiere publisher of print and digital books. Our concise and applied books are for...

- Professionals and Practitioners
- Faculty who adopt our books for courses
- Librarians who know that BEP's Digital Libraries are a unique way to offer students ebooks to download, not restricted with any digital rights management
- Executive Training Course Leaders
- Business Seminar Organizers

Business Expert Press books are for anyone who needs to dig deeper on business ideas, goals, and solutions to everyday problems. Whether one print book, one ebook, or buying a digital library of 110 ebooks, we remain the affordable and smart way to be business smart. For more information, please visit www.businessexpertpress.com, or contact sales@businessexpertpress.com.

Printed in Great Britain
by Amazon

54429670R00067